THE
ME
I NEVER KNEW
I COULD
BE

THE
ME
I NEVER KNEW
I COULD
BE

RANDI LESNICK

BOOKLOGIX®
Alpharetta, GA

ISBN: 978-1-6653-0276-0 - Paperback
ISBN: 978-1-6653-0277-7 - eBook

Library of Congress Control Number: 2021918185

Printed in the United States of America   0 9 0 9 2 1

♾ This paper meets the requirements of ANSI/NISO Z39.48-1992 (Permanence of Paper)

Author photo by John Drobin

To Allen:

You were my friend, lover, caretaker, and business partner.
I only wish we had more time . . .

To Jason and Jonathan:

You are the best of both of us. I will love you forever!

To Robin and Robert:

Thank you for the strength you gave me to continue
on my journey of life!

To Andrea Williams:

A special thanks for helping me through the emotional process
of finding the words that fill these pages.

PROLOGUE

I left the Franklin house in a haze of grief. I couldn't stay there anymore. I couldn't continue to walk by the pool every day, remembering just months prior when, under a blazing August sun, my husband and I had splashed our feet in the water like younger versions of ourselves, amazed by the people we'd become. "Can you believe this is our life?" Allen had said. He was smiling. He seemed so happy.

But now he was gone. For good. And even though I would never see him again, would never sit next to him on the couch and tuck my body into the side of his, I still felt him everywhere. I could feel him when I went to bed at night and when I woke to make coffee in the early morning hours. His spirit was also in the gazebo just off the pool that served as his outdoor man cave, the place where he could smoke his cigars freely while watching the Preds play. To be clear, that was never the intended use for that space. Ten years after we built the house, after the pool had been installed, I envisioned having dinner parties in that gazebo, perhaps serving tiramisu beneath its thatched roof. But that was before Allen claimed it as his own, hanging his neon signs and stocking his favorite beer in the mini fridge.

Truthfully, I didn't mind this hijacking. The space seemed to make him so happy, and, ultimately, the Franklin house was the beautiful and perfect manifestation of all our dreams. It was where Allen and I raised our two amazing sons, Jason and Jonathan. It was where we built a business and a future, where we planned to stay as we watched that company, and our kids, grow into more than we could ever imagine.

Then Allen left, for good, and it was all so much—too much— and I couldn't stand it. His absence suffocated me. It was thick in my chest, like smoke from a fire; it hung like anchors on my limbs. I knew I had to leave that home we made together in another, happier, time. But I couldn't.

It was my sister who eased me out the door. She flew in from New York and promised not to leave until I was better, or at least until I could convince her that I was. She knew that I was trapped in limbo, so her first order of business was to find me a new place to live, one that didn't have Allen's memory built into its foundation.

We drove around to look at homes in the suburbs of Nashville, or, more aptly, she drove and I stared out the window, trying to make sense of the new world whizzing past my tear-blurred eyes. A world without Allen. We saw places in Brentwood and Green Hills and eventually settled on a condo in the new CityLights development downtown. It was just steps from the Ascend Amphitheater, and the sales brochure felt fitting for a vacationing bachelorette, not a grieving widow: *Panoramic views, modern amenities, stylish interiors, and all the people and places of America's newest "it" city waiting just outside your door.*

I can remember, vaguely, walking through the first-floor unit that would eventually become my home. There were three bedrooms—one that would become my office and one that would serve as a guest room for my sister or one of the boys if they decided to sleep over. And there was the master, of course. It was a large, spacious room at the back of the condo with the type of floor-to-ceiling windows that make blackout curtains a necessity as the sun began its daily ascent. It was stunning, just like the Franklin house, but it was not home.

In retrospect, I should have said no, and I should have demanded that my sister take me somewhere else. There was no room for Trixie and Duke there, not really—not like the large yard we'd left in Franklin. Each CityLights condo had a balcony that was little more than a rectangular piece of concrete that jutted out from the building and overlooked a smattering of other buildings. But there was no green, no place for the dogs to run or jump or have anything close to what they did before. I saw all of this but said nothing. I smiled, instead, and I told the realtor how *beautiful* it was.

———————

Three months later, after weeks of being frozen by grief, I'd finally moved into the condo. It still didn't feel like home yet, but the dogs and I were making it work as well as we could. I unpacked clothes and hung pictures of Allen, me, and the boys; meanwhile, Duke and Trixie followed me everywhere. For me, their constant companionship required as much of an adjustment as moving to a downtown condo as a widowed woman of sixty-two. It was Allen whom the dogs used to trail behind, all but ignoring me. Now, without Allen, they sat at my feet while I answered emails; they paced the kitchen floor while I made the coffee in the mornings. If I grabbed my purse and started heading toward the front door, they hurried to catch up, pressing their bodies against my legs, willing me to take them along. They didn't want to be alone either.

We kept up this precarious existence as best we could, taking things one day at a time, as all the grief manuals suggest you should. Then, in early March, Jason told me he finally was coming over to look through the coin collection he had inherited from Allen. He was going to check their value on the internet, take what he wanted, and leave me with all that he couldn't carry. I told him to come early. I knew that sorting through the coins was going to take a while, since my approach to packing up the Franklin house was simply to find boxes large enough to toss in armfuls of stuff with little review or organization. This is how I had cleared out the contents of our safe, where Allen had kept his coins and all of the other important documents and materials gathered over thirty years of marriage.

I'd only been back a couple weeks after visiting my sister in New York when Jason came to collect his coins, when he also found the letter that would change everything. At that point, the shutdown was imminent but not in effect. The whispers were there, the rumors coming out of China that something was amiss. But here in Nashville, kids were still in school, and restaurants and bars were still open. The music, like the beer, was flowing freely from the honky-tonks on Broadway. Everything was still normal—for some people, at least.

I was in my bedroom when Jason came, and I stayed there as he began the task of sorting through all the things that would make me remember. I didn't want to remember, not then, so I remained far enough away to control my own emotions, to prevent myself from breaking down in tears at the slightest memory. I'd been listening to Jason rummage through boxes for a couple hours, hearing the sounds of clanging coins and rustling papers, when he called out for me.

"Mom," he said, "I found something."

Jason's voice was shaking, as if he were demanding it not to break. I knew then that this wasn't another coin he'd found. This was something else, something serious.

I tried to keep my breath steady as I walked out of my bedroom and into the sitting area where Jason was waiting, but it was so, so hard. My heartbeat had already quickened, and there wasn't a shred of optimism left in me. Not after the last four months we'd endured. After all, it had been just weeks since I'd been able to sleep through the night without waking up in tears; it was even more recently that I'd learned to finish a full plate of food before pushing it away in disgust, my body heaving with so much hurt and pain that I couldn't squeeze in another bite.

What more could there be? I thought as I approached my son. *What new storm has blown in to wreck our lives again, tearing away the last few strands of rope that were barely holding us together?*

As I got closer, I could see the paper in Jason's hand, white and trifolded. It was a letter, I realized, but from whom? My instinct was to take it from him immediately, but he stopped me before I could. He placed a hand on my arm and said, "Mom, you better sit down for this."

Reluctantly, I sat. Then, letter in hand, I unfolded it and started reading:

> *Dear Love of my Life:*
>
> *If you have to read this letter, I am sure it will be extremely painful for you and the boys. But as a responsible father I have to leave you these guidelines so you can move on with your lives.*

I felt my stomach lurch. Allen had written a letter the morning he passed away, but it was nothing like these neatly typed pages. The other letter was handwritten and nearly incomprehensible. Why would Allen write that letter if he'd already written this?

> *First and most important, Randi, don't do anything for the first six months. It will take that long to get your head back together.*

I looked around the condo, at the brand-new furniture I'd bought after deciding to leave everything but the art in the Franklin house. "I don't want any of it," I'd told my realtor. "Just sell it all."

I blinked, and the water welling in my eyes fell in heavy drops onto the paper; my chest rose and fell sharply. I knew that Allen knew me well, even better than I knew myself, but holding the proof of his devotion in my hand shattered my heart all over again. He was the love of my life, now gone, but he'd thought enough to prepare me for a life without him.

For two pages Allen wrote his instructions in explicit detail: *Pay off all the credit cards and medical expenses and pay off the Chrysler Town and Country. Do not pay off the house.* He wanted me to set up six different mutual funds; he told me who to go to for financial advice; he even gave me homework. *I know you hate to read about finance,* he wrote, *but you must read two books for me.*

I could hear Allen's voice as I read his words. They were stern but gentle, and I realized that he didn't just want the boys and me to survive once he'd left—he wanted us to prosper. At the top of the second page, I also realized something else: Allen hadn't written that letter in October 2019. He wrote it in 2000, two decades prior.

I dropped the papers and watched them flutter to the floor as knowing swept over me. It felt like the closing scene in a movie, right after the climax, when the main character begins to understand how every moment that came before had brought him to that place, at that time.

In an instant, my mind raced over the last twenty years. I thought about every time that Allen seemed despondent or unlike himself. When we got married, I knew he'd been taking antidepressants since before we met, and there had been an incident when the boys were still young that brought his illness into searing focus. He'd stopped taking his meds for a while, and his depression had shown up ugly and unwelcome. But we'd fixed it. At least, I thought we had. He started seeing a therapist, and every day after that, I reminded him to take his medication.

But as I read his letter, I realized that we hadn't ever fixed anything; all at once I understood that he had suffered for twenty long years. As a husband and father, his commitment was to take care of his family—in life and in death. I could only assume that, at some point after writing the letter back in 2000, he decided that Jason, Jonathan, and I still needed him. The instructions, while thoughtful, must not have been enough, or maybe he didn't trust that I would follow them to the letter. But whatever the case, he waited. He waited, and he suffered, and he helped me build a successful business that he knew would provide for me and the boys.

I was shocked to discover that Allen had even considered suicide many years ago, when we still had so much ahead of us—our children growing, our business thriving, our family prospering. It was both surprising and saddening. Still, in spite of it all, I could take solace in one thing: he didn't do it.

For twenty years, suicide wasn't an option. And then, it was.

CHAPTER 1

Allen and I were never supposed to be together. Susan, our mutual friend who fancied herself a matchmaker in her spare time, had been trying to get us together for weeks. Unfortunately for Susan, Allen had already told her that he wasn't interested in a blind date. I felt the same—even though, truthfully, I didn't have many other options.

After living in Florida, Texas, and Alaska for work, I finally moved back to New York in 1988. My mother and sister were thrilled that I was finally closer to home, never mind the fact that I had only moved because I thought I'd found my future husband, a man that I'd met at my sister's wedding. I was working in sales and marketing for Hilton at the time, but the company wouldn't transfer my move back home. As a result, my boyfriend and I dated long-distance just long enough for me to sell all my belongings in order to finance my move. When I finally resettled on the East Coast, I had my whole life mapped out in my mind; the wedding would come first, of course, then there would be kids. They would grow up with my sister's kids, and we would spend Saturday afternoons in Central Park picnicking with our whole extended family.

By April of 1989, none of that seemed possible anymore. My relationship had met its unceremonious death, and I'd spent the previous six months placing personal ads in the *New York Times,*

1

voluntarily subjecting myself to the horror of one blind date after another. I would, on purpose, schedule multiple dates on the same day: a breakfast, a lunch, a dinner, and sometimes, cocktails. I'd learned quickly that the threat of having somewhere else to be was the most seamless way to escape a bad date, and trust me, all of them were bad. I remember coming home after making small talk with the last guy—a banker from the Upper West Side who spent the whole meal talking about his family's boat—slamming my front door shut and collapsing against it with a promise to never date again.

Once I swore off personal ads, meeting a friend of a friend didn't sound too appealing either, even if that friend was someone I genuinely trusted. But Susan wouldn't take no for an answer.

A few weeks after she first tried to convince me to go on a date with this anonymous friend of hers, she called to ask if I wanted to go to party with a big group of mutual acquaintances. When I agreed, she threw in the kicker: the party was going to be at Twenty-Second and Park Avenue, and there were people coming in from Westchester, New Jersey, and Long Island. Since my place was the closest to the party, Susan decided we would all meet at my apartment at 8:30 p.m. and head over together.

The night of the party, I got ready early and tidied up in case anyone wanted to come in for a drink. When I heard a knock at my door at 8:30 on the nose, I knew it wasn't Susan, who was always late for everything. I just hoped that the stranger liked red wine and that it wouldn't be long before the rest of the group showed up.

I opened the door and looked up into the face of a tall, nerdy guy with large lapels and a bottle of Chardonnay clutched in his hand. He told me his name was Allen, and I smiled and said hello. If I had entertained Susan's matchmaking efforts even slightly, I might have asked for her friend's name. If I'd done that, I would have realized that the man standing in my doorway was the man in question.

I invited Allen in, pulled stemware from my cabinet, and poured our drinks. Then Allen and I talked, and we talked some more. We talked about the schools we'd attended, as well as the fact that we both worked in the hotel business. All of it was so effortless, so all-consuming, that I never realized how much time had passed.

When the phone rang two hours later, Susan's voice brought me back to the present.

"So, what do you think?" she said.

I pressed my ear against the phone and listened for background noise—horns blaring or tires screeching—and when I didn't hear anything, I realized she hadn't called me from a pay phone. In fact, I was starting to think she may not have even left home yet.

"I think you're late," I said, fully frustrated. "Where the hell are you?"

Susan just laughed in that airy, nonchalant way she so often did. "I'm not on my way to your apartment," she said. "I'm calling to see how everything's going with you and Allen."

"Excuse me?" I asked, slowly putting everything together.

There was that laugh again. "I wanted you to meet Allen and I wanted Allen to meet you, and since neither one of you were willing to go on a blind date, I had to figure out another way to get the two of you together."

We'd been set up.

I looked over at Allen, at the bottle-and-a-half of wine we'd already finished, and I hung up the phone. If Susan had called even an hour before, I may have been a little upset. By that point, however, Allen and I were knee-deep in the get-to-know-you phase. We were drinking, talking, and enjoying spending time with each other; the fact that we were technically on a blind date was of little consequence.

I will say that if there was anything about Allen that gave me pause that first night, anything at all, it was his constant sniffling. He'd say a few words, then sniff. Nod his head in agreement with me, then sniff. Months later, once we were an official couple, I understood how seasonal allergies hijacked his life every spring and fall, but on that night in 1989, I actually thought he was a drug addict. I even asked him about it that night.

"Seriously," I said, "are you on cocaine?"

Allen laughed and said no, that pollen was the culprit behind his constant nasal drip. His response seemed logical enough, so with the important stuff out of the way, we decided to meet Susan at the party, but only after stopping for dinner. I can't remember where we went or what we ate—Pasta? Steak?—but I recall what happened next quite vividly: we walked over to the party, and before we went in, Allen bent down and kissed me for the first time. It was everything I could have hoped it would be—passionate, gentle, a promise of something more.

Allen and I only stayed at the party for about ten minutes before returning to my apartment. The next morning, I called my mother and told her the truth that had been burrowing itself into my heart from the moment Allen's lips pressed against mine at the corner of Twenty-Second and Park Avenue.

"Mom," I said. "I met the man I'm going to marry."

———————

After that first night, Allen and I were inseparable. There were no games, no concerns about whether either of us was calling too often or coming on too strong. By the end of the year, we were taking our first trip, a drive to Vermont to stay in a bed and breakfast where we would celebrate the end of '89 and ring in a new decade together. The plan was to do the standard bar crawl through town on New Year's Eve; we'd already purchased our tickets and were looking forward to clinking our champagne glasses at midnight while we hugged other sweaty revelers that we'd never met. But first, we needed rest. After we checked in to the B&B, we laid across the queen-size bed in Room #1 and drifted off to sleep.

I guess we were exhausted—me from my work as the regional director of marketing for Hilton's Suburban Hotels, and Allen from his Marriott job in catering—but we didn't open our eyes again until the winter sun started to peek through the curtains of our room on the morning of January 1.

We laughed about it that morning, how we'd planned our entire vacation around the midnight celebration and then slept right through it, but I also thought about what that night had meant for our relationship. I realized that I didn't care that I'd missed New Year's at all. In fact, I couldn't think of a single thing that I would have rather done than spend the holiday curled up in bed with him. And since I'd made up my mind about Allen, I had to know if Allen had made up his mind about me.

We were driving back to the city and hadn't been on the road more than ten minutes when I turned and asked him flat out, "Is this relationship going anywhere?"

Allen drove silently for a moment before responding, "What do you mean?"

"I'm thirty-three years old, and I don't want to waste any time," I said. "Are we going to get married? Have kids? I need to know."

I watched the contours of Allen's face while he watched the road stretch out in front of us. I've always been impulsive, the type to act first and ask questions later. But Allen, always the analytical type, was the exact opposite. He researched and pondered and mapped out a plan before making any big decisions.

Finally, he nodded his head and said, "Yes, you're right. We should get married." He paused before adding, "I don't have a ring yet, but I'll take care of that. In the meantime, I don't want you to say anything to anyone. Not even your mom or your sister. I want to get you a ring, and I want to do this right."

I said, "Yes, of course," and thought back to that first morning after I'd met Allen, how I'd called my mother and predicted that Allen and I would get married. I was giddy and grinning, and the first time Allen stopped to get gas, I rushed to a pay phone to call my mother and tell her that I'd been right all along. My stomach was still hot with excitement when I crawled back into the car and Allen was there, staring, his eyes asking the only question that mattered.

"I'm sorry," I said, "but I had to call my mom. She won't care about the ring; she'll just be happy that I'm happy. And I'm *so* happy."

Allen was pissed, but he understood and still agreed to go with me to dinner with my family once I got back in town. Over Peking duck and sweet-and-sour chicken, my mom and sister asked Allen dozens of questions. I'm sure he assumed that I'd already told them everything about him (I had), but for the sake of pleasantries, he answered every question anyway. He didn't speak much of his family except to say that he and his sister had always been close, especially after his mother's death. He talked about his job with Marriott, how he enjoyed the hotel business but thought he may be better suited for another side of it, perhaps sales. He thought he'd be good at it, even though he didn't love the idea of having to talk to strangers on a regular basis. Allen wasn't exactly shy, but he was certainly slow to warm up to people. As he was talking, I held his hand under the table, silently showing him my love and appreciation.

After dinner we went back to my place, where we celebrated our engagement and the beginning of the rest of our lives together. We went to sleep together; we woke up together. It was all so perfect, I thought.

Then Allen disappeared for three weeks.

———

For nearly a month, I didn't see Allen, and I didn't talk to Allen. I didn't even talk to any of Allen's friends who may have known his whereabouts. I was heartbroken, naturally, that the man to whom I'd just gotten engaged had slipped out of my life without so much as a warning. But at thirty-three, I didn't have it in me to chase him. He was the one who'd walked away, so if he was going to come back, he needed to do so on his own accord. In the meantime, I threw myself into my work and told my mother and sister not to worry. Finally, when it seemed that Allen may have been gone for good, I decided to call.

"Look," I said, bluntly, "I don't know what's going on with you, or with this relationship, but I've had it." I paused and waited to see if Allen was going to interject, to maybe explain where he'd been and what he'd been doing. When he said nothing, I continued, "I was very open about what I need in a partner at this point in my life, and this isn't what I'm looking for. This just isn't working for me. We need to talk."

Allen agreed to come over the next day, and before he arrived, I was all set to break up with him. I'd gathered his belongings that he'd left at my place and put them neatly in a bag. I'd resigned myself to the fact that I may have been wrong, that I probably wouldn't be spending the rest of my life with him after all.

When Allen finally knocked on the door, I had the whole conversation planned. I knew exactly what I was going to say and how I was going to say it, because I'd already rehearsed it several times. My words were going to be direct, but not the least bit sentimental. There would be no room for misinterpretation—I was ending it once and for all.

I let Allen in and offered him a drink, but before I could turn to the kitchen to get it, he reached out, grabbed my arm, and told me to wait. Then he dug his hand into his jacket pocket and pulled out a ring—his mother's ring.

"Randi," he said, "will you marry me?"

I gasped. This was not what I was anticipating, or what I had prepared for. We were supposed to be breaking up. I'd already packed his shirts, his toothbrush, a couple of books he'd left on my coffee table . . .

"Yes!" I said. "Of course, I'll marry you!"

Allen smiled, relieved, and wrapped me in his arms. It was like the previous three weeks had never happened, like we'd awoken the morning after our engagement and spent the next weeks picking out wedding colors. But that wasn't the truth, no matter how much I'd wanted it to be. We'd, instead, spent the last twenty-one days on opposite sides of the city, not speaking to one another.

I pushed myself back and let air fill the space between Allen and me. I had agreed to marry him, but I still needed answers.

"What the hell happened to you?" I asked.

Allen shrugged, but not in an uncaring, insensitive way. He looked dejected, like someone who couldn't explain his behaviors because he couldn't understand them himself.

"I was scared," he said, finally. "I freaked out. I thought about my dad. He was a terrible husband and a terrible father, and I thought I'd end up like him."

For the next few minutes, Allen told me more about his family than he ever had before. He told me how, shortly after his mother's passing, his father had married the nurse who had been helping to care for his disabled sister, Vivian. He told me that his father's new wife hadn't wanted Vivian as a child, so Allen had been left to care for her alone, even though he was still just a teenager himself. He'd done the best he could for three years before going to his aunt and uncle, begging for help. Allen and his sister eventually moved in with them, but the heavy load that Allen had already strapped onto his back remained there indefinitely. He'd grown up much faster than he should have, and ever since then, he'd worried that he was somehow broken because of it, that maybe he'd become the person who broke others.

My heart hurt watching Allen share his deepest hurts. I had no way of knowing just how deep the pain was, or that he would carry some of that pain for the rest of his life. I only knew that I loved him more than anything. I wanted him to know that, and I wanted him to know that none of his past mattered to me, that I would stand by his side no matter what.

"It's funny," I said, grabbing Allen's hand and moving closer to him, "but I was going to break up with you today."

Allen raised an eyebrow. "Really? Is that how you still feel?"

I smiled, and before I could say another word, he leaned down and kissed me, just like he did at Twenty-Second and Park Avenue.

CHAPTER 2

Like so many girls growing up in the '70s and '80s, I started smoking cigarettes when I was still a kid. I was seventeen, and every time I inhaled a chest full of nicotine, I saw myself as cool and alluring, as sexy as all the glamorous movie stars who walked around with long, thin cigarettes hanging from their puckered lips. Back then, we didn't have the pictures of a healthy lung next to a cancerous one, all shriveled and marred with dark spots, to alert us of the dangers of our disgusting habit. Back then, you could go to the fanciest restaurant in town, order a hundred-dollar steak and finish it off with an after-dinner cigarette in the middle of the dining room.

As I got older and moved from my late twenties to early thirties, times started changing, and people became more aware of the health risks of smoking. There also seemed to be more people who didn't smoke and who didn't want smokers around them. Allen was one of those people.

I was a clean smoker, or as "clean" as you could be, considering. I washed my hands constantly and blew smoke out of windows. If I was at home, I stepped outside to avoid filling my apartment with the stench of my cigarettes. Even still, Allen hated it. He could smell it on my clothes and taste it on my lips, and before we got married, he told me that he wouldn't stand for it anymore. For Allen, my smoking was the deal-breaker that could end our relationship for good. So, like any anxious soon-to-be bride, I obliged. Or, more correctly, I lied.

"I promise," I told him days before our wedding. "Once we get married, I'm never going to have another cigarette." As soon as Allen and I said "I do" and walked back down the aisle, smiling at family and friends who had gathered to see us become man and wife, I politely excused myself. I told Allen that I needed to freshen up, that I'd be gone five minutes, tops. I stopped in the room where I'd gotten ready just an hour before and quickly sifted through my things until I found what I needed. Moments later, I was in the restroom, taking long drags and awkwardly twisting my head so the smoke wouldn't be absorbed into the lace and tulle of my wedding gown. I loved Allen more than anything, but even my love for my new husband couldn't convince me to quit smoking cold turkey.

The only thing that could was my love for my son. When he was five years old, Jason came home from school one afternoon with his face long and his eyebrows knotted with worry. "Mom," he said, "I talked to my DARE teacher about you today. I'm scared that you're going to be sick from smoking."

It was the '90s, and schools across the country were implementing Drug Abuse Resistance Education courtesy of the Los Angeles, California-based nonprofit. The country was knee-deep in the War on Drugs by then, and like every other mother, I was in full support of any program that would prevent my kid from becoming some strung-out junkie on the street. I assumed that Jason would be taught to avoid drugs like heroin and cocaine, that he would learn how even casual experimentation could send you down a spiral that would impact the rest of your life. I wanted my son to be scared of *those* drugs, the kind that could rip you from your family and leave you on the corner begging for loose change. But for Jason, there was nothing more horrifying than a mother who smoked Marlboros.

"My DARE teacher told me that I need to keep praying for you to stop smoking," he told me. "And I am praying. I'm praying every day for you to stop smoking, but it's not working. Nothing's happening."

Even now I can remember Jason's eyes, wide with genuine worry.

"You know what," I said. "Your teacher's right. I want you to keep praying to help Mommy stay strong, 'cause watch what I'm gonna do."

I walked over to my purse and pulled out what was left of my last pack of cigarettes. I shook them into my hand, all eight of them, and I made a tremendous spectacle out of breaking them in half and then throwing them into the trash can, one by one. I looked over at Jason, whose worry had turned to skepticism even as he nodded his head in approval. I smiled, too, even as uncertainty swept over me. I also said my own prayer for strength and resolve. Almost twenty-five years later, I can't say whether it was Jason's prayers or mine that made the difference, or perhaps a combination of the two, but they worked. I never had another cigarette again.

It's actually fitting that it was Jason instead of Allen who convinced me to give up smoking for good. Everything with Allen was so easy, starting with our first conversation in my New York apartment, so I may have subconsciously avoided anything hard that he asked me to do. Having children, however, was a challenge from the beginning. It was one fight after another, long days and longer nights, so many of them tear-soaked. Eventually, the moments of searing pain led to my two sons, and that, I know, gave me the grit to overcome any difficulty I would face while being their mother—even giving up smoking.

———

Allen and I knew that we wanted kids right away. I had just turned thirty-four when we were married, and time was of the essence. Thankfully, *gratefully*, I found out I was pregnant just two months after our wedding day.

The day of my positive pregnancy test, I decided to surprise Allen at work. I waited outside his office and called for him to come down to the parking lot. My heart was thumping wildly in my chest, and when he came to the car, I was doing all I could to mask my anxiety. I grinned and handed him the balloons I purchased from the grocery store. Then I told him the news. Allen was a serious man most of the time, but when I told him he was going to be a father soon, his face relaxed with joy.

I had, of course, already told my mom and my sister. Like the news of our engagement, I couldn't bear the thought of not telling them first, and like the night of our engagement, Allen was upset about my apparent refusal to honor his role as my husband. "You should have told me first," he said. Perhaps he was right, and I had overstepped again. But even this disappointment couldn't dampen our elation. We were going to become parents, transferring the best and worst of ourselves to a tiny human who we hoped would one day become all that we had never been.

─────────

It is rare that moments of heartbreak unfold slowly, giving you time to process and plan. In most cases, life upends in the blink of an eye; one moment everything is fine—good, even—and the next, it is not.

Allen and I were at home at our co-op in Hartsdale, New York, when the spotting started. Even though the blood came slow at first, it was enough to cause concern. I was five months pregnant then—too far along to dismiss my soiled underwear as benign. I pulled out my copy of *What to Expect When You're Expecting* and flipped to the second trimester. I quickly scanned the words, but only as a matter of technicality. I didn't need to read the book to know that something wasn't right.

"I think I need to see the doctor," I told Allen, who was sitting on the bed next to me. In what would become the routine of our lives, he took control, gently but firmly, and grounded me with assuredness.

"Okay," he said. "I'm sure everything is fine, but let's go."

Allen and I moved quickly, but so did the blood. Within a couple hours, it was flowing thick and heavy; I switched from a panty liner to a maxi pad, and the blood soaked through that too. Still, when we arrived at the ER I was deliriously hoping for the best, praying that it could all be explained away, that a magic pill would dry up the blood and my tears. Hours later, an ultrasound confirmed the worst: I'd had an ectopic pregnancy and my fallopian tube had ruptured, filling my abdomen with blood like water rushing into a capsizing canoe.

The doctor didn't think I was going to make it, so he called my family to advise them to come and see me while they still had the chance. The blood was high like the tide by then, reaching all the way to my diaphragm. I remember seeing my mother's face just as they wheeled me into the elevator to take me down to the operating room. It must have been right before they put me under because I later learned that my procedure began before I even made it to the operating room. I was suffocating in my own blood, the doctors told me, and the only way to relieve the pressure was to slice me open, right in the middle of the elevator.

Research suggests that one in every fifty American pregnancies results in ectopic pregnancy and that certain risk factors, including smoking, can increase those odds. What's more, for women who have had one ectopic pregnancy, the chance that the next pregnancy will be ectopic is 15 percent. I'd had my first ectopic pregnancy when I was just nineteen and living with a guy who I dated for five years. When I moved away and started traveling the country for work, we drifted apart, and I was able to cast that pregnancy in a different light. Suddenly, I didn't have to be shackled to a man who wasn't right for me, a man from my past. I could have never imagined, however, that the echoes from that pregnancy would reverberate into my future.

When I opened my eyes after my surgery, I was still groggy

from anesthesia and pain meds, but I could hear the doctor loud and clear. He leaned in close and whispered, "There's always adoption." I could tell that he intended his voice to be soothing and encouraging, that he wanted me to feel okay about the removal of an entire fallopian tube and ovary. But my brain didn't register that. It was only hours before that I had been lounging at home, reading and making plans for dinner while my baby grew inside me. It had all changed so quickly, far too suddenly for Allen or me to effortlessly switch gears.

My mom was there in the hospital, and so was my sister, who had adopted her own two children. They tried to console us too, but I was hysterical, adamant. We wanted to have our own babies.

I hated IVF from the very beginning. The daily injections were painful, and Allen hated giving them to me. They also sent my hormones into a tailspin. I was still working—at that time, I was consulting on a new hotel that was to be built in Brooklyn—and while the work itself wasn't hard, reeling from what felt like a near-constant state of PMS made everything more difficult.

On top of that, there was no way to know if the treatments would even be successful. There were so many risk factors, and even in the best of cases, rates of a successful IVF pregnancy could be as low as 25 percent for women around my age. Odds do improve with each cycle, though, so I kept pressing forward, even when Allen wanted to quit. And to be clear, Allen wanted to quit after our very first round. In addition to wanting to prevent me from going through any more pain or discomfort, he had begun to get nervous about the idea of our child inheriting his allergies and family history of mental illness. We hadn't talked about it, but I knew that Allen took an antidepressant daily. As long as he stayed on top of his meds—which, at that point, he did—I didn't worry about it. In fact, I didn't even think about it. Allen, obviously, did.

I was still dead set on giving birth, so I kept pushing for more treatments, and two rounds later, we had invested thousands of dollars in the hopes that I would soon give birth.

I was driving on the New Jersey Turnpike on a clear weekday afternoon when I got the call that that wasn't going to happen. The next day, I was scheduled to have an egg retrieval—they were going to collect eggs from my remaining ovary and then fertilize them with Allen's sperm before implanting them in my uterus. But there was a hiccup, the doctor told me. My estrogen levels had fallen drastically, indicating that I was likely a low responder with too few egg-containing follicles to justify a retrieval. He apologized, and my appointment was canceled.

The doctor was nice enough, and he offered to continue with fertility treatments in hopes that my levels would rebound. Reluctantly, I declined. In that moment, I knew that all my chances of having my own child were gone. We weren't going to spend any more money; I wasn't going to ask Allen to give me any more shots. That was it. After countless hours in clinics and even more time spent wondering and worrying, it was all over, and I had no baby to show for it. Hysterical, I pulled over at a gas station on the New Jersey Turnpike and bawled.

I called my sister, knowing that I was unfit to drive. Twenty minutes later, she arrived and took me to her house where I sat in a rocking chair in her daughter Dana's room, waiting for Allen to come. I must have sat there for hours and hours and hours, just crying and crying and crying.

Meanwhile, as I suffocated in my grief, my sister called the consultant who'd helped her adopt her children. A couple days later, when I'd had time to collect myself and began looking toward a future without a child whom I'd physically birth, Richard Gittleman, the consultant, called.

"Are you done trying to duplicate yourself?" he asked. "When you are, let me know so I can adopt a child for you."

It took only a couple months for Richard to find the mother who would give birth to our child. He knew everything about her.

He'd already screened her and talked to her several times; he knew that she had had all the proper tests and was healthy; he knew that she was taking the steps to ensure that the baby would be healthy too. Allen and I agreed to move forward with the adoption, and just that quickly we were filled with hope again. We signed the necessary documentation and wrote the necessary checks. Then, in November 1990, we traveled to meet our son Jason and bring him home.

We arrived a few days after Jason was born on November 14, and we assumed we'd head back to New York a few days after that. Instead, I stayed for months in a two-story-hotel suite, waiting for the Interstate Compact papers to be signed so I could leave with my new baby. Family and friends came to visit as Thanksgiving gave way to Christmas and New Year's. Allen eventually had to leave to go back to work, but as January turned to February, I received the signed papers and was allowed to go home.

It was early 1991 when I arrived back home in New York, and along with the pages of the calendar, time had washed away every trace of the anguish I'd felt just months before. I was a mother, finally, and my baby, Jason, was perfect.

CHAPTER 3

When we brought Jason home, Allen and I were still living in his one-bedroom co-op in Hartsdale. It was a decent enough place—certainly good enough for a single man, and perhaps doable for a young married couple. But it wasn't sufficient for a family of three. I had already fixed up the place as much as I could, adding curtains and flowers and generally trying to make it look like more than a bachelor's pad. The biggest change, however, was adding the nursery.

I had always dreamed of having a nursery for my baby, and I couldn't wait to create a room where Jason would sleep and play, a room that would illustrate my deepest love for him. I painted the walls a shade of pale yellow and added a wallpaper trim that depicted animals walking into Noah's ark, two by two. The furniture—a crib, dresser, and changing table—was all-white and anchored on a rug that matched the walls perfectly. And in the corner was a rocking chair nearly identical to the one in my niece's nursery at my sister's house, the same chair that held me as I mourned the loss of any chance of bearing my own children. Now I would sit in my own rocker, holding my own baby, so grateful that I could still become a mother.

The nursery was beautiful, but it was also built in our apartment's only bedroom, which meant Allen and I had nowhere to sleep. When I first told him about my plan—and the fact that we would have to sleep on the pull-out couch in the living room—Allen met my eyes with confusion in his own. Still, he said nothing. I don't think he understood why I would give up our bedroom, but he did understand why I felt that I needed to.

Even at that early stage of our marriage, Allen was my biggest fan. It is often said that opposites attract, and, indeed, many marriages are built on a union of contradictions. There is the spender and the saver, the night owl and the morning person, the hot-tempered and the cooler head. In my relationship with Allen, there was the impulsive idea machine and the calm, cautious supporter. It goes without saying that I was the former, Allen the latter.

———————

When Allen's aunt began bringing us gourmet chocolates from her travels in Belgium, it was my idea to start a company that would import Belgian chocolates and then sell them, in bulk, to companies looking for corporate gifts for their clients and employees. In my mind, success was all but guaranteed. I had a few connections of my own from working in the hotel business for so long, and I leveraged every single one. I also tapped into my mother's connections and did a good bit of cold calling to amass a client list that could net a healthy profit margin. As the orders started to come in—first in a slow trickle but, eventually, in a steady stream—we rented an empty apartment directly below ours to maximize space. It became the fulfillment center for our growing business.

I recruited family and friends to help package and label the candies, but most of the time it was Allen and me—with Jason on my hip—boxing orders into the wee hours of the night. Allen worked at Stouffer's during the day and became the candyman during nights and weekends, but never once did he complain. Never once did he tell me to do something less strenuous or suggest that I focus my energy on being a mother. Allen understood that, like my own mother, I was a career woman. He also understood that having a child only made me *more* determined—not *less*—to make a name for myself and to help Allen build a life that we could all be proud of.

About a year after starting the chocolates company we moved to Briarcliff Manor, to a townhome with enough space for Jason to have his own room. Around this time, Allen also purchased a special lamp that was designed to help with depression.

At first glance, it looked like a traditional light fixture, but the bulb had been designed to mimic the sun's rays and carried a measure of illuminance that was nearly ten thousand times the standard household light. These lights are sometimes prescribed to people who experience seasonal affective disorder, or SAD, which is a type of depression that is brought on, or exacerbated by, a lack of sunlight. SAD is most prevalent in fall and winter, when the days get shorter and the sky cloudier. And in northern parts of the country like New York, where winter can stretch into April and fall begins knocking on the door in mid-September, SAD can make it increasingly difficult for someone who suffers from depression year-round to keep their condition in check.

I didn't know what triggered Allen's depression at that point in our marriage—we still hadn't talked about it—but I watched him sit in front of his lamp each day, closing his eyes and tilting his chin toward the ceiling as if he were sunbathing on a beach in Hawaii. Did it help him? It's hard to say. Back then, I just didn't know what I didn't know. I didn't know what it looked like for someone to spiral out of control.

Once we moved into our new place, I decided to pivot in my new career as an entrepreneur. Allen was busy working as the director of sales at Stouffer's, and I was busy chasing Jason around while trying to keep up with a new consulting gig. I'd left Hilton when the company decided to move its regional office to Atlanta and gave me the option of relocating or walking away with a golden parachute.

I decided to stay in New York and raise my son, and when Muss Development, the company that owned the new hotel, learned I was leaving Hilton, they decided to keep me on board as a consultant. Working and parenting a toddler was a full load in itself, so I hired a housekeeper to help me keep the townhome clean. She also happened to be a fantastic seamstress.

Maria would show up to our house in shirt-and-pants combos that she had designed and sewed herself, and with each outfit, I was blown away by her skill and attention to detail. At the same time, I was always carrying around an extra change of clothes for Jason in case he spilled ketchup or juice or splashed into a muddy puddle when we were visiting friends. Maria regularly sewed clothes for her family, but it wasn't long after she made her first outfit for Jason—a pair of bright blue overalls—that the idea came to me to start a business with her help.

We would develop a line of reversible kids' clothes called Funny Stuff, perfect for busy moms like me who would rather be meeting with clients than doing another load of laundry. Now, a soiled shirt wouldn't have to be immediately removed and stuffed inside an overflowing diaper bag; it could be turned inside-out, and any stains would be instantly hidden from view. I thought the idea was genius, and I (correctly) assumed that other moms would think it was genius too.

Maria and I were an efficient, effective machine. I invested the money to buy fabric and other supplies, and she designed and sewed all the clothes. Later, once we had some solid samples, I took them around to local boutiques and convinced the buyers that Funny Stuff was the hottest new thing in children's apparel. To drive my point home, Jason wore nothing but Funny Stuff clothing for a solid two years. He was our toddling billboard—a built-in brand ambassador before we knew what that meant—and sometimes I even took him with me on sales visits. The buyers would grin and coo at the cute kid in his color-coordinated clothes; then, when it was time for the big reveal, I would pull his shirt over his chubby stomach and arms and flip it around to reveal a whole new look. We worked for a while this way—me, Maria, and sometimes Jason. All the while, Allen would watch from the sidelines, always cheering me on, always ready to offer a helping hand.

Like the Belgian chocolates company, Funny Stuff was born on a whim and hunch, as well as a belief that I could build a successful company from scratch, even while being a wife and mother. I had lots of ideas back then, primarily because I knew that no matter how long I had prayed and waited to become a mom, I could never be just a mom. I needed something more. The chocolate company and the kids' clothes were my most successful attempts at creating something more during those early days of our marriage, but no matter how unproven or seemingly farfetched my ideas, Allen supported them all. In return, I pledged to always support him too.

It was a phone call that put this promise to the test, the moment that called into question my commitment to each one of our wedding vows.

"Are you sitting down?" Allen asked on the other line.

I had just taped up a box of new Funny Stuff vests and jackets when the phone rang. Cradling the cordless phone in the crook of my neck, I quickly carried the box to the front door and left it there so Allen could easily transfer it to the car when he got home. Finally, I sat down on the sofa in our nearby living room. "Yes, I'm sitting," I said. "What's up?"

"My job got transferred, and I have my choice of cities to transfer to."

I sat up straighter on the couch and pressed the phone tighter to my ear. "Okaaaaaay," I said cautiously. "What are the choices?"

"Chicago, Orlando, or Nashville."

I'd spent much of my career in the hotel business traveling and working in different places around the country, but Allen and I had never discussed the prospect of having to move for his job.

Suddenly, I felt foolish for not ever considering the prospect that Allen would potentially have to leave New York, but I shook this thought from my mind. I wanted him to know that I supported him no matter what.

"Well, that's great!" I said. "I'm okay with moving. Wherever you want to go, just let me know."

Allen cleared his throat. "That's good," he said, "because I already chose Nashville."

Without a second thought, I hung up on him.

I could imagine myself in Orlando. The weather was nice, and we'd be close enough to the beach to take Jason on a regular basis. Even Chicago, with its winters as cold and unforgiving as New York's, would have worked for me. Despite being in the Midwest, Chicago was a big city with a sophisticated sensibility and all the trappings of East Coast life. But Nashville? I'd never even heard of Nashville.

I quickly got Jason dressed and strapped him into his car seat so we could drive over to our local library. We rushed through the front door and hurried past the information desk where I found it: a globe. I located Tennessee, a skinny, rectangular state about halfway between New York and Texas. It wasn't as far away as California or even Kansas. But neither was it DC or Massachusetts. It was far, and it was in the middle of nowhere—at least, nowhere I had a desire to be.

Holding Jason, I thought about my family, about leaving my mom and my sister, and having to live hundreds of miles away from them while I raised my new baby. The idea made my stomach tighten. In my heart, I didn't think I could leave them. But I also knew that if there was one thing that could change my mind in a hurry, something that could convince me that the move was in the best interest of our family, it was the possibility that we could buy a house in our new hometown.

The cost of living in New York was, as it has always been, through the roof. So even though Allen and I were both well-established in our careers and making good money, we knew that it would be a while before we were financially stable enough to buy a home—at least the kind of home that I wanted to live in. I had watched as my mother built her own business and crafted the lifestyle she desired—both glamorous and built on her own terms—but I also knew the sacrifices she'd had to make in the process, as well as how long it took. I had fully inherited my mother's drive and perseverance, but I'd be lying if I said that I was prepared to work another twenty years before I could experience that kind of freedom. More than anything, I wanted a house for my son to grow up in, perhaps some outdoor green space where he could run around and play. And if moving to Nashville could help me get that sooner rather than later, I was happy to go along for the ride.

While still in the library, I called the International Chamber of Commerce and asked about the cost of living in Music City. The gentleman I spoke with explained that if the median cost was 100 percent, New York came in at more than 200 percent; Nashville, meanwhile, was 94 percent. I was sold, and I hung up the phone to immediately call Allen.

"You find me a house," I told him, "and I'll move to Nashville."

Allen had only two weeks to report to Tennessee. That meant two weeks to pack, two weeks to say goodbye to friends, two weeks to visit my favorite restaurants and cafés around town. Eventually, I started getting excited about the move, but the timeline made me nervous. Nothing, however, prepared me for what happened next.

It was a couple days before Allen was scheduled to leave and a storm swept into New York that blanketed the city in snow and ice in a matter of hours. I'm from New York, so I know snow, but this was like no snow I'd ever seen. It came so hard, so fast, and there was no way to prepare. The night that it started, with the temperature dipping into the twenties, all the pipes in our townhouse busted, and within moments, the bottom level was flooded. It was the middle of the night, and Allen I were in knee-high boots, wading through the icy water that came up to the middle of our shins.

The next day, I went to my mother's to stay with Jason while Allen made his final preparations to leave. We'd put all our belongings in storage, and I tried to remain positive, to not view the storm as some kind of eerie omen. Then, a few weeks after the flood, long after Allen had finally boarded a plane at LaGuardia, I turned on the news and heard the latest weather report. New York was expecting another storm, the meteorologist said, and we could see up to twenty-four inches of snow. I couldn't even bear the thought of it, so I packed up Jason and we left for Tennessee immediately.

———

When we moved to Nashville, we lived in two adjoining rooms at the Renaissance Nashville Hotel, where Allen was working. There was no kitchenette in our room, so we ate downstairs in the hotel's restaurant and Renaissance paid for everything. Meanwhile, Jason had chicken pox, broke his shoulder jumping on the bed, and spent most of his days running his Hot Wheel cars alongside the windowsill in our hotel room. The arrangement wasn't convenient, to be sure, but I didn't care. My focus was on my family.

Allen and I were ready to adopt again, to give Jason a younger sister or brother. We knew the process by then. We knew about the consultant's involvement and what needed to be done before the adoption could be completed. Most importantly, we knew about the home visit. And at the time, we didn't exactly have a home.

Almost immediately after arriving in Nashville, Allen had found a house that he just knew I would love. He had a realtor give him a tour and he recorded the interior and exterior before mailing the video to me in New York. I never got the video, though, because he'd sent it just a couple days before I'd packed Jason up in haste, so determined was I to get to Tennessee before the next storm rolled in. Now that we were together, Allen could take me to the property and show me in person.

We drove to the neighborhood in Bellevue, just west of town, and toured the subdivision's model home. I loved it, and we decided to have our own house built there. I was giddy with excitement thinking about the decorating and hosting family during the holidays, and I couldn't keep from smiling when I realized that we would have a garage, backyard, and a porch. This thought kept me energized as I visited the site with Jason each day and went back again with Allen in the evenings. Finally, I had a new project to work on, something tangible and worthwhile to fill the void that closing my businesses had left behind.

But building a house wasn't just about having a new place for Allen, Jason, and me to call our own. Building a house also meant having a place where we could have our next home visit and, ultimately, welcome our new child.

The only problem? Building that house was going to take nine months.

CHAPTER 4

We fell in love with our new home right away. In addition to having space to spread out and neighbors to swap recipes with, there was a new school, Harpeth Valley Elementary, being built nearby. It was the new pride of Metro Nashville Public Schools, and Jason would be among the first group of students admitted. Overall, Metro Nashville schools weren't great, but we were excited about Harpeth Valley and the new principal and the teachers who would come in and give all our children a world-class education. Our plan was to stay in Bellevue until Jason finished fourth grade. Then, right before he would have to start middle school, we'd move further south to Williamson County, where the schools were better. In the meantime, we prepared for Jonathan.

Almost immediately after arriving in Nashville, I'd called Richard, our adoption consultant. Jason was almost two then; we had bonded and were close, and I felt ready to have another baby. I'd always known that I wanted two kids, and I knew that I wanted them to be close in age. My sister and I were close—just two years apart—and it shaped our lives from an early age. Childhood bickering aside, she was the one I could always turn to even if the whole rest of the world turned against us. We grew up together and learned from each and I wanted Jason to have that same experience.

In a perfect world, Allen and I would have had our second son a few months after arriving in Nashville, but learning that we had to be in our new house to schedule the home visit altered our timeline considerably. Needless to say, I called the Nashville office of the Catholic Charities to schedule our home visit as soon as the moving trucks pulled out of our new driveway. We then spent the next couple months feverishly unpacking and making Jason's room and the new baby's nursery just right. The whole house was immaculate, but we wanted the Catholic Charities representative to take particular note of the way we cared for the child we had and the way we planned to care for our newest one.

Once the visit was completed, we called Richard. I was nervous—like I had been before, like I was through every step of the adoption process with both of my sons—but Richard assured me that everything was fine. Then, nine months later, quite ironically, he called and asked if I was ready to be a mother again. All the emotions I'd felt before I met Jason for the first time came rushing back. I was full of anticipation and joy, still anxious but also settled, calm.

My mother and aunt flew into Nashville to stay with Jason while Allen and I hit the road to go pick up our new son. The Interstate Compact papers were already signed—we'd learned what not to do during our first adoption—so all that was left to do was go and meet Jonathan. We didn't want Allen to have to take off too much time from work, and even more important, we didn't want to have to leave Jason for very long. So, we spent one night in a hotel and then boarded a plane the next morning, three parts of our new family of four. When we arrived back home, Jason was standing in the garage and holding a homemade banner in his chubby little hands that said "Welcome Home Jonathan," and finally, I felt like our family was complete.

———

Over the next year, we slipped into our new routine: me staying home with the boys while Allen went to work at the Renaissance.

I don't remember how long we'd been married before I realized it, but Allen was never really happy in the hotel business. He had a hotel management degree and was good at his job, whether he was working in catering or sales, but he hated selling. He hated making small talk with people on sales calls; he hated making sales presentations to large groups. More than feeling nervous about talking to strangers, it was the phoniness of it all that bothered him. He hated having to talk to people with the sole goal of getting something out of them. Still, he stayed in the industry and was always willing to do what he felt he had to, for the sake of our family.

I don't attribute Allen's unhappiness with his job to his depression, mostly because he'd battled the disease well before we ever married. But I can't deny that it must have weighed on him to show up day after day to a job that didn't make him feel happy or fulfilled. I think he might have been disheartened that, even after moving to Nashville, his job was essentially more of the same.

He'd been so excited about the move, the change in scenery, and in some ways that change was beneficial. Sometimes, and certainly in Allen's case, family members can come to represent pain and struggle far more than love and security. For Allen, even though his job was still full of monotony, I think leaving New York presented an opportunity to leave the most awful parts of his past behind so that he could focus fully on building a more beautiful future.

Did Allen love the fact that our condo flooded right before we left, that our first place in Nashville was two adjoining hotel rooms, or that we had to live in that hotel for almost a year while our house was being built? Probably not. But Nashville was still new, an opportunity for a fresh start. This is how I thought he saw things at least, but if I'm being honest, I must admit that, at least in the beginning, I was so busy trying to make the most of our abnormal living situation that I didn't have much time to think about how Allen was managing it all.

I was chasing Jason around the hotel and trying to adjust to not having my sister or any friends around. Not only were we in a brand-new city, but there weren't any other women in the hotel for me to talk to, certainly not anyone who was staying on a long-term basis like we were. But through it all, I made sure to keep my glass poured half-full.

I remember walking with Allen and Jason from the Renaissance down to the banks of the Cumberland River that snakes through downtown Nashville. It was empty there at the riverfront and all around it; all we could see was a glow from the neon lights outside the honky-tonks on nearby Broadway. It's remarkable to consider what Nashville is today—the "it" city and country music capital of the world—and then to remember what it was just thirty years ago. Back then there was no professional football or hockey team, nor were there James Beard award-winning or Michelin chefs coming to town to set up shop. Nashville was a city on the cusp then, just as we were a family at the beginning of our trajectory, with nothing but hope and opportunity stretching out far in front of us.

My sister came to visit soon after, and she didn't quite have the same view of the city that I did.

"There's no culture here," she said to me. "Are you sure you want to stay?"

I said yes, of course, and not just because we had to live in Nashville because of Allen's job. I knew that I wanted to stay because I had a feeling that something great would happen for our family in Tennessee, that we could plant roots here that would blossom into something more beautiful than we could have imagined. In short, I always assumed the best. I assumed that we'd be okay as a family, and I assumed that Allen would be okay too.

Later, after we moved and brought Jonathan home, I also assumed that Allen was healthy and at least somewhat happy—mostly because he made it so easy for me to do so. Allen was so great at slapping on a smile, wrapping his arms around me, and convincing me that everything was fine—even when it clearly wasn't.

———————

Jonathan had been home for about a year when I started noticing that Allen was acting strange, despondent. I watched him move in near silence for weeks. Every day was more of the same: he got up early for work, came back home, spent a few minutes with the boys, and then went straight to bed. I waited for him to snap out of it. I waited and waited until, eventually, I couldn't wait anymore.

"Are you okay?" I asked over dinner one night. Allen was moving his food around the plate with his fork, making circles in his rice, while staring off into the distance.

"I'm fine," he said, without looking up.

"I don't think you're fine. You certainly don't *seem* fine."

After a few more minutes of silence, Allen finally looked up at me. And in his eyes, I saw a terror—a panic—that I had never seen before.

"I don't think I can do this," he said.

In that moment, I reached out and wrapped my hand around his. I didn't have to ask what "this" meant, nor did I have to wonder why he felt so overwhelmed. I'd felt it too—the pressure of balancing baby and toddler, the go-go-go of days that ran headfirst into sleepless nights. I'd sat with the worry of bringing up children in a world with constant uncertainty and danger, and I'd questioned my ability to lead my sons through it. In many ways, I think this is common among parents; in fact, I think it's what makes the best parents so good. They want to be the best and do the best for their children, so they question every single decision. So many of us do this, but what Allen was going through was something altogether different.

Allen had seen what parenting looked like in its ugliest, most-selfish form. As a child, he was saddled with pain and struggled to come out on the other side in one piece. He knew what it meant to have a parent who didn't put him first and didn't do everything in his power to make the world just a little bit easier. He had a parent who, instead, actually made things harder. As a result, the scars of his youth caused him to worry that he would be become that kind of parent himself. Allen worried that even with his commitment to family, his tireless work ethic, and his sacrificial nature, his past would still be impossible to outrun.

That night at dinner, my heart broke for my husband. All the sun lamps and daily pills had alerted me to the fact that there was a problem somewhere, that he wasn't as perfect as I had willed him to be in my heart. Even still, the day-to-day of life, work, and babies had made it easy to overlook his struggles. In the process, I inadvertently pushed whatever darkness had been lurking in Allen's mind to the far corners of mine where I never had to confront it. Suddenly, though, it was right there, sitting in front of me and making my sweet husband question his abilities as a father.

"Have you been taking your meds?" I asked.

He shrugged and glanced away. "I started feeling better, so I stopped."

In an instant, my mind clicked back through the previous year, how we'd finally moved into our house and finally brought Jonathan home. There was so much to be excited about, so much to be thankful for, that maybe, even in the overwhelm, he felt happy for once. Or maybe it was the pills themselves that had created a sense of equilibrium and normalcy so strong he felt that he no longer needed antidepressants. I have no way of knowing, but I do know that in his state of relative joy, he'd failed to anticipate the shorter days and longer nights of winter and how the excitement of a new house and a new baby could eventually give way to boredom and frustration.

"Well," I said, already getting up from the table, "we need to find you a new psychiatrist who can give you a new prescription. We need to get you back on track."

I am a fixer, and the only thing I know how to do is fix things. I knew that I couldn't fix Allen completely, but I believed that I could fix his current pain, even if only temporarily. So, for the next few months, Allen's mental health was all I focused on. I made sure he was taking his meds, eating right, exercising, sleeping well, and doing everything else I could to help him feel better.

All the efforts were effective, but as Allen started to feel like himself again, I started to realize that I wasn't feeling like myself. I was sitting on the floor one day, playing with the boys as *Barney* blared on the TV screen above us. It was a moment I had prayed for years before, a moment that I wasn't sure I would ever have as I recovered in the hospital after my ectopic pregnancy. But suddenly that moment wasn't enough. I needed to get back to work.

Before I got married, I managed twenty-four suburban hotels as the regional director of marketing for Hilton Hotels. I was ambitious and career-minded, and I had the success to prove it. Later, after Allen and I brought Jason home, I was still working and making money, this time on my own terms. I could take care of my baby and still launch a profitable business. It wasn't until we moved to Nashville that I found my hands empty for the first time, my calendar filled with playdates and pediatrician checkups instead of business meetings and site walkthroughs.

This transition was fine for a while. When we lived at the hotel, I was focused on getting our house built and then preparing to bring Jonathan home, and all those things kept me extremely busy. Then, suddenly, we had the house and our family, and I felt . . . lost. I loved my babies more than anything, but I couldn't shake the emptiness I felt from having left such a huge part of myself in the working world.

I cried that day as Jason and Jonathan sang along to *Barney*. Hours later, Allen walked in and found me still lying on the floor, still mourning my former career. Despite his personal struggles that he was still working though, he picked me up, dried my tears, and started putting together a plan to help me address mine. Allen knew as well as I did that, I'd be a better mother if I got back to work in some capacity. Any money that I earned would be ben-eficial, of course, but he knew I was never driven by that. I was driven by my desire to create something successful, something that was far bigger than me.

Soon, I would have that opportunity again.

CHAPTER 5

First things first, Allen and I decided that we would put the boys in the day care at our local temple and that I could work part time or full time, so long as I could pick up the kids and be back at home by three. This was more my decision than Allen's. Once he knew that I was serious about getting to back to work, he supported me fully and would have never tried to restrict what I was able to do. But he didn't have to. Working was important, but it was never more important than my children.

I thought back to my mother and how, when my sister and I were little, she worked as a substitute teacher. It didn't pay extremely well, and it certainly wasn't a lifelong career choice for her, but it was a role that allowed her to get out of the house and earn her own money without taking over her life. She could be there when we got out of school in the afternoons and during the summers, and that was exactly what I wanted for my boys. I wanted to work, but I also wanted to be with them as much as possible.

With the boys' care squared away, I turned to the next, and most critical, task: finding a job. Under normal circumstances, I would tap my personal connections before I turned to the classifieds, but having recently moved to Nashville, my Rolodex was predictably slim. Thankfully, after working at the Renaissance for a year, Allen did know enough people that he didn't think it would be too difficult to find something for me to do, especially with my years of experience.

The first meeting Allen set up for me was with a woman named Helen Moskowitz, who owned her own destination management company called Moskowitz and Associates. We hit if off fine, and the interview went well enough . . . until it was time to discuss salary.

"You have to keep this between us, because nobody else is getting this," she said, leaning across the table toward me, "but here is what I'll pay you." With her perfectly manicured fingers, she slid a folded piece of paper in my direction, just like in the movies. That act alone sent a current of excitement rippling through my stomach. I always believed that people wrote down the offer when the number was too big to say out loud. When I picked up the paper and looked at it, I realized that, in this case at least, the opposite was true. Helen must have written that offer down because she wouldn't dare let a number as pitifully low as $25,000 come out of her mouth.

Without hesitation, I declined. I had been making six figures in New York, and while I understood the difference in cost of living between New York and Tennessee, I certainly thought I was worth more than a quarter of my former salary. I didn't know what I was going to do next, or even if I'd get another offer, but I knew that I couldn't sell myself that short. So, I walked.

While I waited for another opportunity, I decided to get more involved in the temple day care where we were sending Jason and Jonathan. As the president, I organized fundraisers for the school, addressed any issues that arose with teachers, and served as the final point of contact for prospective parents who were considering enrolling their kids. The position kept me busy, I got to see my kids whenever I wanted, and I still had time to look for another job. As it turned out, I wouldn't have to look very long because, about two months after I first met with her, I received a call from Helen Moskowitz.

Helen was working with a client who was preparing to buy out the entire Opryland theme park to host an event for their employees and clients. The point person for the client had called and told Helen that she'd heard I was in town. "If Randi handles this account and oversees the event, I'll keep the account with you," she told Helen. "Otherwise, I'm moving to another agency."

Helen didn't want to lose the client because she was building a pool at her home and couldn't afford to return the fee that the client already paid her. She had no choice but to call me, and she had no choice but to pay my full ask of $65,000. It wasn't my full New York salary, but it was enough to live on in Nashville. It was also much more than she'd offered me before.

For a couple of years, everything was perfect. My work-life balance was great—I was able to pick up the kids at three every day, just like I wanted—and, initially at least, I thought Helen was wonderful. She was dynamic and assertive, and I saw myself learning a lot from her. The more I actually learned, however, the more I realized that she wasn't such a great leader after all. Eventually, I walked away, once again prioritizing my integrity over any paycheck.

I went back to being a mom and welcomed the temporary break as a chance to plot my next step with real intention. I'd done great work for Helen and had started to make a name for myself around town, so I knew I wouldn't be without a job for long. I had my own contacts at that point, so even if no one reached out to me to offer a position, I had plenty of people I could call, plenty of people whose companies would be made better if I worked there.

But before I took that step, I needed a moment to think. I needed to figure out what I could do that I would really enjoy, something that I would be really passionate about. I needed to do something big.

———

The scene was not unlike any four-year-old's birthday party: About a dozen hyperactive boys were running circles in a suburban backyard with just as many half-eaten pieces of birthday cake strewn across a table. Jason was having a blast playing with his friends from temple; Jonathan, on the other hand, was having a horrible time.

The vomit had come out of nowhere, as it often does. I was covered in it, and poor Jonathan was screaming inconsolably, his face bright red. I was in the guest-of-honor's kitchen, trying to figure out how to get myself clean and get Jonathan quiet when a voice called out from behind me.

"I'm just dying to tell someone."

I turned to find a dark-haired gentleman grinning widely. He seemed oblivious to both the still-crying toddler in my arms and the wretched smell that was emanating from my shirt. "I'm selling my imprint," he continued, "and I'm starting a brand-new record label."

Suddenly, the man had my full attention. I had no idea about running a record label, but I knew it sounded exciting, and I knew this man was someone I needed to get to know.

"That's amazing," I said. "Tell me more."

The man shook his head, so eager to share his exciting news. "It's a country label, and we've got offices right on Music Row. We've even signed our first two acts already."

My knowledge of country music was limited to the songs that were played on the radio, but it didn't take a rocket scientist to know that Nashville was the country music capital of the world. Country music was the engine that drove a large chunk of the town's economy, and it was, as far as I could tell, the "Music" in Music City. If this man was going to be working in country music, he had to be doing something big. And if he was going to be doing something big, I wanted to be a part of it.

"You're kidding me," I said. "That's *so* cool." Jonathan's head was knocking wildly against my chest as I bounced him on my hip, silently begging him to get quiet. He must have known that something important was happening because, in an instant, his screaming stopped.

"When is the official launch?" I asked the man.

"Maybe August or so," he said, still smiling. "It's going to be amazing, and I'm going to have a huge grand-opening party."

I have replayed that scene in my mind countless times since it happened in the spring of 1996, but not once have I been able to figure out why I saw this stranger's grand-opening party as the big opportunity I'd been looking for. Somehow, though, I knew it was. I knew that a door had swung open, and I was determined to leap through it.

"What a coincidence," I said. "I actually plan parties for a living!"

I had never planned a party in my life.

Sure, I had thrown dinner parties with my friends in New York and hosted birthday gatherings for the boys, but I had never done anything like this. This wasn't just a party; it was the grand-opening celebration for the hot new record label in town.

It was a big deal, and no matter what it took, I was going to figure out how to convince that man to hire me as the planner. Allen and I were still pretty new to town, and we knew absolutely no one in the music industry, so there was no one we could call to put in a good word for me. I wanted him to know how creative and hardworking I was, how professional and easy to get along with, but since there was no one else to tell him for me, I knew that I needed to tell him myself. And since he wasn't exactly the easiest person to get in touch with, I knew that I had to keep calling him—every day, for three weeks—until I could tell him.

Every day, for three weeks, I called. Every day, for three weeks, I heard nothing.

Then, at seven in the morning on a sunny Tuesday, he called me back.

Of all the times he could have called, that was probably the least ideal. The kids were sleeping and could have woken up at any moment; our dog, Casey, was outside and would start barking when she was ready to come back in; and Allen was in the shower getting ready for work, unable to help if anything had gone awry.

Despite all of this, I never considered not taking the call. It was my only option, my only chance to land this amazing gig. If I told him that I would call him back, he may have never answered, and I just couldn't take that risk.

I shut myself in our walk-in closet, crouched beneath Allen's work slacks, and tried to sound as natural as someone whispering in a closet can sound.

"So good to hear from you," I said.

I expected a greeting in return, but he skipped the pleasantries. "I can't stand it anymore," he said. "You've got to stop calling me. You're like a fucking Jewish mother."

I paused, unsure how to react. Was he calling just to tell me this, to tell me not to stalk him anymore? Immediately, I started formulating an explanation in my head. I wanted to apologize for being so aggressive, but aggressively was the only way I knew how to go after something I really wanted.

"Look," I said, "I can explain—"

"What's the name of your company?" the man said, cutting me off.

"Excuse me?"

"Your company? You plan parties, right? What's the name of your company?"

I didn't have a real business yet, and I was kicking myself for not thinking about this during all those days I spent ringing his phone off the hook. Now I needed a name, and I had no time to think. I'd worked as a consultant in the hospitality business, so maybe . . .

"Hospitality Consultants," I said quickly. "My company is called Hospitality Consultants."

I gave him my home address as the official headquarters of the company next. Then, in one more stretch of the truth when he asked for my business phone number, I casually replied, "I'm in the office now. The number you just called is my business line."

"Great," he said. "Now, just stay on the phone and listen."

The line went dead for a second, then I heard ringing.

For the next ten minutes or so, he made call after call, letting his industry colleagues and vendors know that I had gotten the gig. "Going forward, please direct all calls regarding the Red Robin grand-opening party to Randi Lesnick of Hospitality Consultants," he explained. "She is our official party planner, so there is no need to call me anymore."

When he was finished, he told me that he wanted me to meet the rest of the Red Robin team in a couple of weeks to go over specifics for the event. I hung up the phone, and as if on cue, Casey started barking wildly, the kids woke up, and Allen stepped out of the shower.

———————

I had no idea how I was going to plan this massive grand-opening party with no professional party-planning experience, but I never doubted that I would. I'd spent my entire life figuring things out and, before that, watching my mom do the very same thing.

When my father had his hernia operation, my mother hired private duty nurses to look after him in the hospital. My father had a roommate who had only days to live, and right before the roommate died, he said to my mother, "Watch out for the eleven-to-seven nurse."

It was an awkward statement to make, and I think my mother must have initially thought that old man was delusional in his last days. Still, she checked it out anyway, and sure enough my mother found gift receipts and other evidence that my father was having an affair with his nurse.

It was a crushing blow, but my mother never wavered in her refusal to be treated like dirt. Even though my mother's income was far from being enough to support herself, my sister, and me, she decided to leave him. More importantly, she decided that she was never going to be financially dependent on any man ever again. She made up her mind in that moment that she would give my sister and me the world and that she wouldn't get married again until she had enough money to put a diamond on every one of her fingers and hire a limo to take her to work every day.

She began working full time, hustling night and day to get her new business off the ground. My sister and I were thirteen and fifteen at the time, and every day after school we would go to a neighborhood diner that kept my mom's credit card on file because that was my mother's way of ensuring that we had a hot meal.

My sister and I were very aware that our family situation wasn't like that of the other kids we went to school with, kids who came home to a plate of fresh-baked cookies and whose mother had dinner ready at five every night, just in time for their father to get home from work. But we didn't care. Even if we didn't fully understand what our mother was doing at the time, we supported her, and we knew that everything she was doing was to take care of us.

My mother's decision to leave my father and build a new career from scratch, even after she'd had children, was all the inspiration and motivation I needed to kickstart my own second career as an event planner. I never once questioned my commitment or ability to succeed; I was raised by a woman who made something out of nothing, and with her blood coursing through my veins, I knew I could figure it out. After all, I'd figured it out in New York, back when I launched Funny Stuff and the Belgian chocolates company.

Before I started those businesses, I didn't know anything about importing candy or selling kids' clothes, but I learned as I went and let my passion and drive guide me to success. Becoming an event planner, I knew, would require more of the same. I wouldn't be able to rely on my connections, education, or experience to get this new company off the ground. All I could do was take one giant leap of faith.

CHAPTER 6

T here was no time to revel in the excitement of my first contract with Red Robin Records. When I hung up the phone after receiving the best professional news of my life, I had only two months to prepare. After having been in business for more than twenty-three years, I now know that putting together an event in sixty days, even an extravagant one, is totally doable. I obviously believed that I could do it back then—after harassing the label executive for weeks, I *better* have believed it—but the only thing I knew was that I didn't have a clue what I was doing. Naturally, I called my mom.

My mother was as clueless about event planning as I was, but she knew how to build a successful business. More importantly, she knew that every success starts with a single action. First things first: I needed an office.

My mom put my stepfather on the next flight from New York to Nashville, and after we said our hellos and stopped to grab lunch, we made a beeline to the nearest Home Depot and Best Buy. He bought some plywood and, back at home, took off the closet doors in the guest bedroom and turned the space into my official headquarters for Hospitality Consultants. Finally, after purchasing a computer and some other office supplies, I was ready to get to work.

A couple weeks later, I was on my way to Music City's Music

Row to attend a meeting with the new staff of Red Robin. I wore black slacks and a patterned blouse and what I lacked in actual know-how I tried to make up for with unbridled confidence. I was the event planner who had never planned an event, but no one could tell by looking at me.

The conference room at Red Robin was completely bare, except for three eight-foot tables arranged in a U-shape. They were stark too, aside from the occasional pen or legal pad scattered across the top. Around the table sat the man who had hired me, a record producer and his assistant, and Paul Christensen, who would later launch Music and Sounds Records.

I introduced myself and told the executives that my family and I had recently moved from New York, and I told them about my previous work with Hilton Hotels. I kept talking, trying to avoid any specific questions they had for me, while playing up the skills and qualities that I knew a successful event planner would most likely have. I told them that I was organized and a stickler for budgets; I also finished projects before or ahead of schedule, and I was super creative. As I spoke, the men were nodding their heads in all the right places, giving me the sense that they believed what I was saying and would trust me to plan their grand-opening event.

Meanwhile, as I was going through the motions and saying what I thought the men wanted to hear, the wheels in my brain were spinning wildly. This event was my chance, my moment, my opportunity to get back to work and to do something new and exciting. I had to get it right—I had to completely knock it out of the park—but I had no idea where to even begin.

These were the thoughts crowding my mind, but then, as if God Himself came down to ease my anxieties, one of the men raised his hand to casually cut me off as I rattled off a couple of event spaces that I had researched before the meeting.

"We're having the event at Ruth's Chris Steakhouse," he said. "We want to buy out the whole restaurant, so you won't have to worry about renting another space or dealing with furniture rental and setup."

Even then, I didn't fully understand what it meant to rent out a space, nor did I have a full scope of what my remaining responsibilities would be when working with a venue that already had its own staff, tables, linens, and food. I did know, however, that hosting the event at Ruth's Chris would make my workload—and stress level—significantly lighter.

I exhaled an inconspicuous sigh of relief. "That sounds like a great plan," I said, with a wide grin plastered onto my face. "Thank you so much for letting me know."

———————

The first real challenge I encountered while planning the Red Robin grand opening was the fact that I had to put down the deposit to hold the space at Ruth's Chris. I didn't understand that this was my responsibility until I called and spoke to a restaurant staffer who told me that we couldn't even begin to plan the event until a check for the rental had cleared the bank.

I knew that this fee would ultimately be Red Robin's responsibility, as they had made the final decision on where to host the event. But I also understood that I was expected to cover the cost initially, even though I could include that expense in my planning fee. The problem was, I didn't have the money.

My mom and stepfather had already been gracious enough to help me with the initial launch for my fledgling business, so I didn't want to ask them for anything else. More than that, though, I knew that money was no object for Red Robin Records, that covering the initial expenses would be no problem for the wealthy business partners. Without hesitation, I called the Red Robin exec who had hired me and told him that I needed to be paid for the party upfront and in full.

"That's ridiculous," he said as soon as the words tumbled out of my mouth. "We don't give full payment in advance."

I strapped on all the poise and tenacity I could muster. "I

understand that this is not your typical policy," I responded, "but this is *my* standard policy. I am grateful to be given this opportunity and excited to work with you, but this is the one condition that must be met before we can proceed."

"I'll pay you a deposit, but that's the best I can do. Besides, our checks have to come all the way from LA, so even if we agreed to pay you upfront, it would probably still be a while before you got your check."

That was it, the window of opportunity that I needed. He'd cracked it just barely, but once I saw that he was waffling, I was determined to bust it all the way open. I had no plan B. Without the check, I wouldn't be able to hire support staff and cover other incidentals, let alone rent out Ruth's Chris.

"Thank you so much for that offer," I said, "but I do really need to be paid upfront, or we won't be able to open the doors the night of the event. This is a really special night for Red Robin, and I want to make sure that it's the best party you've ever attended in your life."

There was a pause so long that I wondered, for a split second, whether I had been too forceful in my ask. Then, a moment later, I heard, "Fine. Let me see what I can do."

I got the check the following week.

For the first Red Robin event, I hired a couple friends, including Connie McCaslin, who had become my first full-time staff member. I didn't really have a grand vision for Hospitality Consultants in the beginning; the plan was to take things step by step, event by event. Connie was happy to go along for the ride. Every morning, she would come over to my house, and we'd sit on the bed in my guest room calling vendors and planning seating charts.

The party was a success, and it wasn't long after I'd put a final wrap on everything that I got a call about my next event for the label. As part of their coming-out efforts, Red Robin was planning to make a huge splash at the Country Radio Seminar, the annual event that brings together people from all corners of country music.

Immediately, I knew that this was going to be nothing like planning the event at Ruth's Chris. If the grand-opening party was a lap around the block on a tricycle, CRS would be twenty-three days in the Tour de France. Just the thought of it was overwhelming . . . and exhilarating. It was technically another event for Red Robin, sure, but pulling it off was going to open up the door to Nashville's entire music industry. Once again, I asked for payment up front; once again, they agreed. Then, Connie and I got to work.

To start, I had to contact the Hermitage Hotel, where the event was being held, to reserve the entire property for Red Robin's staff and clients. My fee was based on a percentage of the event expenses, but I still wanted to negotiate a rate that was as low as possible to prove to the label that I would always put their needs first. For that reason alone, I kept quiet about the fact that I was working with the new label in town that was owned by the ambitious exec I'd met at the birthday party. If the Hermitage had known that, they would have probably charged me double.

Once the reservations were squared away, it was time to plan for the actual seminar. CRS took place over four days and three nights, and Red Robin wanted to have a unique event each night. There was a movie night and a casino night that featured staged poker, blackjack, and roulette tables in one of the Hermitage's ballrooms. Finally, we planned a *Rocky Horror Picture Show* night to pay homage to the 1975 cult classic. All attendees were told to dress up in corsets, thigh-high stockings, and other movie-themed attire, and to take their seats in our makeshift theater in time for the screening that would begin at midnight on the dot. I'd already draped blackout curtains around the room to create the perfect ambience; all I had left to do was start the movie projector once that clock hit twelve.

I remember pacing the hallways of the hotel in the hours before the movie was to start, silently willing time to speed up just for me. It was the last day of the seminar, and, truthfully, I was spent. Considering all the setup I had to do before CRS started, along with registration and event management once the seminar started, it's no surprise that I hadn't slept for an entire week. Halfway through, Jonathan broke his arm and had to be taken to the hospital in Bellevue. I drove across town to meet him there and once I found out he was okay, immediately returned to the Hermitage. I was running on fumes, and even if I had tried to close my eyes, even to take a quick nap, it wouldn't have done any good. There was always something else that needed to be done; my massive to-do list was constantly flashing behind my eyelids.

That's not to say I didn't have help—I had lots, in fact. Unlike the Red Robin party at Ruth's Chris, the Hermitage Hotel didn't make their own staff members available to help work the CRS registration table or facilitate any of the other activities for which I was responsible. As a result, I had to enlist my own support team. In addition to the friends who helped with the party at Ruth's Chris, my mom flew in from New York and even Allen came to pitch in after he got off work at the Renaissance. Everyone was clad in a Red Robin sweatshirt, my own little army of hospitality consultants to perfectly embody my company's name.

Just minutes before midnight on the last night of CRS, I started making my way back to the screening room while simultaneously fantasizing about how long I was going to sleep once the event was all over. After the *Rocky Horror* showing, there would be a bit of clean up that night, then some breakdown after the event concluded the next day. I was so close to the finish line, I got giddy with excitement as I stepped onto an elevator, walkie-talkie in-hand. I had a team of people working for me, but, in all things, the buck stopped with me. I was the one responsible—in fact, I was the only one who could push the button to start the projector for the movie—so no matter where I went, I had to ensure that I could be reached at all times.

As it turned out, having that walkie-talkie clutched in my hand just minutes before midnight proved to be a blessing. Once the elevator doors closed in front of me, a week's worth of exhaustion closed in on me, tight like a vice. I felt my legs go limp and my mind go dark. And in the next moment, I collapsed.

Someone from my team heard my body hit the floor of the elevator and they rushed to meet me once the doors opened back up. I don't remember anything about that moment—about being pulled from the elevator or propped up against a nearby chair. All I remember is the warm liquid sliding down my throat as they filled my mouth with espresso. In quick order, the caffeine rushed into my bloodstream, and I was able to wake up long enough to make it to the screening room and start the projector.

———

CRS was the most difficult thing that I had ever done in my life, but every single moment of it, even the moment when I collapsed on the Hermitage elevator, was worth it. I proved to Red Robin—and to myself—that I could execute a massive, multi-day event, and I did such a great job that I started getting calls from other labels in town who wanted to hire me to help with their events. More important, though, was the fact that, during that four-day, three-night event, I earned enough money to support our family for at least six months.

I had long known that Allen was unhappy working in the hotel industry, that his heart was rooted in finance and investments. But soon after CRS ended, I began to understand how much his unhappiness had morphed into dislike, and even hate. He dreaded going to work in the morning; then, when he got home in the evenings, he'd pore over stock market updates and the latest issue of *Investor's Daily* before crawling into bed and trying to lift his spirits for the workday ahead.

The day that I told him I couldn't take it anymore and I wasn't going to let him spend another day of his life doing something he hated, he had come home from work soaking wet. He'd delivered a presentation that day, and the sweat-inducing anxiety had literally drenched his clothes. That was it for me. I told him that he needed to quit, that neither the money nor the insurance was worth his sanity and happiness.

He hesitated, of course. As a husband and father, he believed it was his responsibility to provide for the family. Meanwhile Hospitality Consultants was just a few months old and far from becoming the business it would later grow into. But I think Allen was hurting enough that even he, who was typically so cautious, saw the benefits of taking his own leap of faith. For this reason, he quit.

Every day for three months, Allen went to the Vanderbilt Library to study for the Series 7 exam that would allow him to become an investment advisor. Throughout the process, Allen's pessimism often got in the way—he questioned whether he'd pass or be able to find a job—but in the end, his preparation allowed him to prevail. Allen aced the exam his first time and began building the career that he would practice until the end of his life.

I also believe that it was during this time that Allen decided to do whatever he could to help me grow my business. He was grateful that I had given him the space to pursue his dreams instead of forcing him to stay at a job he hated, but more than that, I think he felt some relief in knowing that, should something ever happen to him, I could take care of myself.

CHAPTER 7

The first time she said it, the first time she referenced Jonathan's eyes with her obvious worry, I was too prideful to listen. Allen's aunt was in town visiting for a while, and as we were sitting at the dinner table one night, she mentioned that Jon's eye seemed . . . crossed. I told her that I didn't understand, that Jon's eyes were perfectly fine, but she said that sometimes, even if he was looking straight at something, his right eye turned inward.

Allen and I had no idea what his aunt was talking about, and, quite honestly, I was offended. I was with Jonathan every day, and I knew that if something were wrong with him, I would have noticed. I would have certainly noticed before his great aunt who lived all the way in New York and had only flown into town for a week. But two days later, right before Allen's aunt was to head back to New York, she mentioned it again. "Look at his eye," she demanded. "It's crooked."

Once again, I ignored it, and once again, I took offense to what, in my opinion, was starting to come across as an insult to my son. That is the only emotion I remember feeling back then, before we knew what was really happening. Allen supported me, but I am not naïve to the fact that his unconditional support had more to do with his love for me than an assurance that Jonathan was actually okay. Even if Allen thought there was cause for concern, my insistence that everything was fine likely made him believe that it was too.

"I am his mother," I persisted. "If something was wrong, I would know it."

In the meantime, as we forgot about Allen's aunt's claims and chose to believe the best about our son, we kept working. Allen was still studying for his Series 7 then, and thanks to our neighbor, Dr. Neil Patel, who worked at Vanderbilt, he was able to spend his days studying in one of the university's libraries.

At the same time, I was continuing to build Hospitality Consultants. I'd nearly killed myself executing Red Robin's CRS activities, but, in the end, my efforts proved fruitful. Not only did I secure the Red Robin account for my company—which meant, essentially, that I had the first right of refusal to plan any and all events for the label going forward—but I also started receiving calls from other labels who had attended CRS and were impressed by the events I'd coordinated. They didn't know that, after getting only a few hours of sleep, total, over the course of CRS, I'd collapsed in an elevator on the last day. All they knew was that I'd executed every detail flawlessly, and every person in attendance had an amazing time.

Starting with Red Robin shortly after the label was launched meant that they relied on me to handle all their events; they never had a reason to hire a full-time events person to whom they'd have to pay a full-time salary plus benefits. I learned quickly, however, that this wasn't the case at other, more established labels.

The first time I sat down with Connie at Giant Records, she told me, flat-out: "I want to work with you, but I can't justify paying you to do what I am being paid to do."

We were sitting in her office, on opposite sides of her desk that was covered in mementos gathered during her career in the music industry. I wanted this account—I was *determined* to get her business—and when she said that she wanted to work with me, I knew the hardest part had been accomplished. My mind started racing as I searched for a solution.

"What if I could figure out a way to plan your events without you paying me a dime?" I asked cautiously. "Would you work with me then?"

Connie stared at me, no doubt thinking that what I'd proposed would be impossible to achieve. "Sure," she said anyway. "If we don't have to pay you, I don't see why we wouldn't work with you."

For the Red Robin grand opening, I'd rented out Ruth's Chris, a fully functioning restaurant, so there was no reason to outsource any of the logistical tasks to outside vendors. CRS was entirely different, though. I had to work with third-party providers for everything from security to catering and linen rentals, and for each company that I hired, there were at least a handful of others who would have also been grateful for the business. As I thought about this, the solution for my Giant Records dilemma began to take three-dimensional shape: I didn't have to charge the labels that had a full-time events person on staff because I could get paid by taking a commission on the business generated by the vendors I contracted.

At this point, I had the weight of some of the biggest brands in Music City behind me, and I believed that leveraging those brands would help me make my case to the vendors I was already working with. I assumed that catering and furniture-rental companies would be happy to give up a percentage of the substantial profits they could earn by helping me to execute events for Red Robin, Giant, Mercury, and other labels. In the end, my assumption was correct. I had no problem selling vendors on my new pricing model; as a result, I had no problem convincing other labels to hire me to plan their events. What started with Giant quickly snowballed. I never had to advertise, never had to cold call. The opportunities just kept coming in.

Business couldn't have been better, but as it turned out, things weren't going so well at home. It took a while for Allen and me to notice, to see Jonathan's wayward eye ourselves. Once we did, I realized that no matter how much my company continued to grow, I would still need Allen more than ever.

———————

When we decided to look into the issue with Jonathan's eye, I was the one who took him to the ophthalmologist. I was the one who had to hear the doctor's stunning, heartbreaking diagnosis.

"Your son has a brain tumor," he said, "and it's fatal. There's no way to operate on it or repair it. He's going to die."

Jonathan was sitting on my lap, four years old and oblivious to the damning diagnosis we'd just received. He looked up at me with an action-figure clutched in his hand and smiled. I smiled back at him, even though, on the inside, my chest felt as though it was bound by a thousand rubber bands. I asked the doctor if he could watch Jon for a moment, so I could step outside to call Allen. Needless to say, I was hysterical.

When Allen met me at the ophthalmologist's office, the fear that had gripped my heart was still tight, even though I'd calmed down enough to breathe regularly again. This minor improvement was of little concern to Allen, however. He was livid that the doctor would even deliver such devastating news without him present.

Once inside the office, Allen scooped Jonathan into his arms and pressed him close against his body. He then turned to the doctor and said, in his voice that was sharp with rage, "This is completely unacceptable. The way you handled this situation was all wrong, and you've presented a tremendous burden for my family. We will be seeking a second opinion, and we will be seeking that opinion from someone who is more attentive to the feelings of their patients."

With that, he grabbed my hand, pulled me up from my seat, and led Jonathan and me out of the office.

Over the next week or so, as Allen and I tried to formulate a strategy for protecting and healing our son, I saw my husband step up as a father in a way that I had never seen. He'd been there for both boy's adoptions, of course, and he'd been by my side through the years of their infancy, the middle-of-the-night feedings plus the hours of crying we couldn't comprehend. But this was different. Allen didn't stand next to me as we fought to keep our son alive. He stood in front of us—me, Jonathan, and Jason—and vowed to protect us from the unimaginable. His confidence gave me the strength to hold onto a faith that seemed to waver with each morning's rising sun. Every day, I woke up ready to fight for Jonathan and our family, and I had to remember that the fight was worth it, that we would prove victorious. Allen made that possible.

After spending countless hours researching eye problems in children, crossed eyes, poor eyesight caused by brain tumors, etc., I called our neighbor, Dr. Patel. I told him everything that had happened, from the first time Allen's aunt had noticed Jonathan's shifting eye, to the ophthalmologist's fatal diagnosis. Dr. Patel promised to help, and he immediately called Dr. Wright, a surgeon who worked at Cedars-Sinai Medical Center in Los Angeles. After listening to Dr. Patel, Dr. Wright felt that Jonathan's eye issues were related to the eyes themselves, not a brain tumor.

"If anybody can fix Jonathan, I can," Dr. Wright said the first time we spoke on the phone. "Jonathan needs surgery, and I've done this same surgery on my own son. If you come out to LA, I promise to take care of Jonathan like he's my own."

When I hung up the phone, I felt myself breathe deeply for the first time in weeks, and all at once, the bands around my chest felt a little looser. We were far from out of the woods, but we had hope and a plan. And with everyone from Red Robin pitching in their airline miles and hotel rewards to help cover the costs for the months we'd have to spend in LA, I knew that we also had an entire team of people backing us. Finally, we had everything we needed to fix my son.

———

After dropping off our bags at a Marriott close to Cedars-Sinai and checking into the hospital for Jonathan's surgery, we had our first meeting with Dr. Wright. Allen sat in a chair holding Jon on his lap, and I sat nearby in my own seat.

"Take out every picture you have of your son," Dr. Wright said.

The request seemed strange—I couldn't understand how Jonathan's neurological issues could be seen in a photo—but Allen and I did as we were told.

"Look at every picture," Dr. Wright continued, "and tell me what you notice."

I was stumped. "I don't know," I said. "What are we looking for, exactly?"

Dr. Wright leaned in close and pointed to a photo of Jon playing with Jason in our backyard. He'd looked up long enough to smile for the camera. "Look at his head," Dr. Wright said. "It's tilted to the side in this photo, just like it is in every photo."

Quickly, I shifted through the stack of pictures in my hands, then I threw those down and grabbed the ones that Allen was holding. I couldn't believe it. In every single photo, my son's head was tilted ever so slightly to the left. I didn't understand the con-nection between his head and his eyes just yet, but I knew that it was something important—something I'd missed.

Jonathan was officially diagnosed with strabismus, the term used to describe any condition in which the eyes are not parallel, and one seems to move separate from the other. For Jonathan, the cause of his strabismus was a lack of the nerves that connected his eyes to his brain. He was born without them, and unless he tilted his head, his eyes couldn't send a clear picture of what he was seeing to his brain. What's more, if he didn't have the surgery that Dr. Wright was recommending, he would have been legally blind within a year.

As Dr. Wright spoke, I thought back to the issues we'd had with Jonathan's preschool, how his teacher would call for circle time and tell all the kids to gather and pass around an item for show-and-tell or listen to the teacher read. Without fail, Jonathan would be sitting far away from the group, as if on his own planet. For so long, we thought we were dealing with a behavioral problem; we never considered that he literally couldn't see the circle.

I looked up at Dr. Wright, tears welling in my eyes. "You said you can fix this, right?"

"We need to put silicone extensions behind Jonathan's eye to help them connect to his brain so that he can see properly," Dr. Wright said, nodding. "It's an experimental procedure, but if you agree to let me operate on your son, yes, I believe I can fix him. The surgery will take about ten hours, but I promise to let you know if anything comes up along the way. And if you want me to stop at any point, I will stop."

I looked over at Allen, to Jon sitting quietly, blissfully ignorant, in his lap. Then I looked back at Dr. Wright. We didn't have another option; he was our son's last hope. "Do whatever you have to do," I said.

Not long after, a nurse came in and gave Jonathan a suppository to put him to sleep. I remember holding him and staring deep into his beautiful eyes as the medicine started to take effect. His eyelids started to droop until, finally, he was overtaken. His body went limp, and I handed him over to the nurse, not sure if I'd ever see him alive again.

———————

The first call from Dr. Wright during surgery came at about the three-hour mark, and my whole body tensed when I was told that he wanted to speak with me. Allen and I, along with my mother, stepfather, and sister, were sitting in the waiting room, trying to keep the worst-case scenario from replaying over and over again in our minds. At least, they were sitting. I was pacing back and forth, back and forth, my feet moving as quickly as my anxious thoughts.

I went to the phone and pressed the receiver up to my ear.

"Your son is doing great," Dr. Wright said. "Please let me continue."

At the six-hour mark, he called again. Again, my stomach seized with knots. "He's doing great," Dr. Wright said. "Please let me continue. I *need* to continue."

By the ninth hour, my nerves were completely shredded. I was awaiting another call from Dr. Wright, not because I wanted to talk to him, but because I had gotten accustomed to the idea that hearing from him meant good news. When he didn't call back again, I felt myself slip into that familiar place of uncertainty and fear.

So, I leaned on Allen. I had been leaning on him constantly—from the moment that the Nashville ophthalmologist told us about the brain tumor to the moment that the nurse took Jonathan from my arms—but the last hour of Jon's surgery was particularly critical. I was losing my resolve, but Allen, despite his tendency toward realism that veered toward negativity, never did. He kept me centered and grounded. He reminded me that our son was receiving the best care possible, that God wouldn't have allowed us to come this far if He wasn't going to see us through.

Once the operation was completed, Dr. Wright wheeled Jonathan into the recovery room. He looked at Allen and me with a giant smile on his face, and he said, "Your son needs to wear glasses for five years, but after that, he will have 20/20 vision."

I collapsed into Allen's arms, relieved and thankful, as we waited for Jonathan to awaken. Finally, his eyes fluttered open. He turned to me, and looked at me, with his head perfectly straight, and said, "Mommy, I can see you."

For the first time since the whole ordeal had begun, Allen started to cry.

CHAPTER 8

No matter how ambitious I was or how much I loved my new work as an event planner, seeing my kids go through health issues or heartache had a way of rendering everything else irrelevant. When we were trying to get Jonathan's eyesight restored and just hoping that he would make it out of his ten-hour surgery alive, no celebrity-filled record label event mattered at all. My focus was on my family, on my children, and even though they are now both grown men, that hasn't changed. If anything, their age has provided confirmation that all of the sacrificing and worrying I'd done over the years was worth it. It took twenty-three years, but I finally heard Jonathan express his gratitude. I only wish that Allen had been around to hear it.

"I don't know where I would be if it weren't for my parents," Jonathan told a family friend while we were boating out on Percy Priest Lake. "I know for sure I would be blind, and I thank God for my parents." Tears were already welling in my eyes, and when Jonathan turned to me, his face full of sincerity, they came tumbling forth. "Mom," he said, "thank you so much for adopting me."

After Jon's surgery, it was a relief to get back to Nashville and to get back to work, to know that, finally, everything was back to normal, and, hopefully, it would remain that way for a while. On the weekend, and sometimes on weeknights, Allen and I used to go to visit Old Natchez Country Club in Franklin, Tennessee, to have dinner and drinks. Our server was a young woman named Faeda. She was bright and cheerful, and she always took good care of us. One night she came over to our table and told me that she had a business-related question that she wanted to ask me. She knew that I was running Hospitality Consultants—I never missed an opportunity to network, after all—and she mentioned that her church was looking for ways to generate some additional revenue.

"Our church is called the Global Café," she explained, "and it's located downtown, right on Broadway. We have a great space, but we're only using it on Sundays. The rest of the week it sits completely empty, and we were wondering if there was a way to use it to make some money. If you could come and take a look at it, it would mean so much."

I told Faeda that I was honored that she would ask me to help her church, and I told her that I would be happy to come and take a look at the space. So, on an early Wednesday morning, Allen and I drove downtown to meet with the pastor of the Global Café. He was nice enough and incredibly welcoming, but what stood out the most to us was the incredible property. It was absolutely unbelievable. There was a giant bar; an open, airy lobby; retail space; and an additional event space upstairs. There was so much room, so many possibilities to throw the most gorgeous functions, and all the pastor and his team were using it for was a once-weekly church service. Moreover, we were standing at the corner of Fourth Avenue and Broadway in the heart of Nashville's tourism and entertainment district. Nashville was certainly still far from becoming the "it" city it is considered today, but it was definitely coming into its own, and we were right in the middle of it.

At the end of the tour, I shook the pastor's hand and thanked him, again, for inviting Allen and me into his church. Then, not wanting to leave without making my excitement clear, I said, "I can absolutely help you guys make some extra money with this space. I will plan and host events, and it won't be any extra work for you guys. I'll bring in my own food and alcohol; I'll hire the staff; all you will have to do is collect the checks for the venue rental."

All I asked the pastor for was the exclusive right to rent the venue. Once that was granted, we had a deal. If I had learned nothing else in the five years I'd been running Hospitality Consultants, it was how to create a win-win proposition. When I first met with Giant Records, I had to come up with a plan that would benefit their company as much as it benefitted mine. I saw how fruitful it made our partnership when I lead with an intent to respect their business model without trying to force them into mine. I learned how to adjust my business model to meet the needs of every client, and I took that approach into the meeting at the Global Café. I told the pastor that I wasn't going to take a dime of the venue rental for the Global Café; I would only, as always, make my money off commissions from the vendors that I used for any events—the food, beverage, furniture rental, etc.

One of the first events that I held at the Global Café was to announce the creation and branding of Six String Records, a new label owned by Paul Christensen and Dustin Carter. The party was attended by a very young Ashley Michaels, and like Ashley's career, that event would prove to be the beginning of a very long and lucrative ride.

About two years into our stint with the Global Café, Jim Hagy of Chef's Market, a caterer that we used for a lot of our events, came over to the Café to tell Allen about a potential business opportunity. He told him that there was an empty building just down the street on Third Avenue and that we needed take a look at it immediately. "It's been empty for a long time, but I just did an event there," Jim said. "It's a great space. I've seen how successful you've been with the Global Café, and if you can do that here, you can do it anywhere."

Allen went with Jim to see the building, and he fell in love. It was downtown, just like the Global Café, but the spaces were different enough that they wouldn't compete. They were two uniquely beautiful spaces, and the addition of this new space would complement our business portfolio.

"Randi," Allen said, bubbling over with excitement, "you've got to call the owners. Use the Red Robin name, tell them what you're doing at Global Café, show them how much money they can make by working with you. Do whatever you have to do, just call."

Allen was a businessman with a business mind, and he was always thinking about expansion, about doing more and making more money. Meanwhile, I wanted to keep my profit margins as high as possible, and the best way to do that was to avoid paying for venue rentals. If we contracted with more venues like we did with the Global Café, not only would I not have to pay for the rental, but I wouldn't have to call venues and try to work around their schedules when we wanted to host an event there. We would control every event that was held within the spaces; even if a client had already hired an outside planner, that person would have to work with me to facilitate logistics. I would secure the food and beverage as well as furniture rentals, and, of course, I would collect a portion of those fees.

This was the sales spiel that I gave to the owners of the new space that Allen had gotten so excited about. "I know you don't know who I am, but my name is Randi Lesnick and I plan events for some of the biggest record labels in town," I said. "I also work with a venue down on Broadway and have helped the owners make a lot of extra money when their space isn't in use. I can do the same for you and it won't cost you a penny."

I had never had to cold call to get clients for Hospitality Consultants, but in this case, and with Allen encouraging me in the background, I was happy to do it. I was taking a giant leap of faith, and I told the owner that he should consider taking a leap of faith with me. The only thing the other would lose was hundreds of thousands of dollars in forecasted revenue.

We signed the contract, and as soon as the ink was dry, Allen and I went back to our staff and gave them the task of coming up with a name and logo. Laurie Hardman, one of my top designers at the time, came up with aVenue. It was a clever play on the words "a venue," and we loved it.

aVenue became the second property in our portfolio, and because of the revenue I was able to generate for the owners, they soon asked me to take over rentals and events for their other properties. When we added Cellar One and Market Street Emporium, we officially launched our newest venture, Nashville Event Space, a conglomerate of venues that generates leads for events.

Ultimately, Nashville Event Space became a massive success, and it was, without a doubt, because of Allen. I had the connections and the vision and the practical expertise in event planning, but Allen was the business savant. He did the marketing and sales; he did the number crunching and all the important tasks that I wasn't great at and, quite frankly, didn't want to do. He understood the importance of getting those things done and was happy to roll up his sleeves and do them himself.

Allen also saw the potential that lay in taking Nashville Event Space online. By building a website that was optimized for keywords, he knew that the company could essentially market itself, especially in the earliest days of the internet. He understood that creating an event-planning and venue-rental company that was fully online would set us apart from what few competitors existed and help us to grow really big, really quick. And he knew that our marketing efforts would make us even more attractive to potential venue partners that would absolutely benefit from the steady stream of event clients that they wouldn't have to lift a finger to get.

In every case, Allen was right. Slowly but surely, I was building a very profitable business, but I couldn't focus all of my time on Nashville Event Space. Hospitality Consultants was still in full swing, and I soon booked an event that would take up even more of my time.

In 2004, I was working with Curb Records when I was asked to do an event for Mindy Dee. I worked with Joe McMin, who, in addition to being an employee of Curb, also served as Sam Thomas's day-to-day manager. Joe was slated to handle the production for Mindy's event while I took control of décor, and throughout the process, he and I became really good friends. Then, once the event was over, he offered me a once-in-a-lifetime opportunity: during the summer of 2004, I was hired to host pre-show meet-and-greets and after-show parties for Sam's Take Out Tour.

I traveled all over the country, to Virginia Beach, Chicago, and other cities too, renting out restaurants and other venues, meeting new caterers, and generally having a great time. It was a lot of work, to be sure, but I was able to bring the kids with me sometimes. During the school year we hired a neighbor named Stephanie to watch the kids until six p.m. I tried extremely hard to be home by three to meet the kids, and Allen would try to make it home by six p.m., but for those times when our schedules didn't align, we had Stephanie. She was also helpful on the weekends if Allen had an appointment and I also had to work, but for the most part, I tried to be with the kids as much as possible, even if it meant bringing the kids along with me. Needless to say, it meant a lot that Sam was so nice to the boys when they came out for a couple dates during his tour.

There was one day that always stuck with me: It was raining out, and the boys, who were ten and twelve at the time, had been planning since the day before to go rollerblading. The weather didn't accommodate, so they spent the morning skating back and forth through the arena where Sam would be performing later in the evening—and they were skating right in the middle of his sound check. I had tried to keep them quiet and still, but since I was in the middle of setting up that day's event, I had failed miserably. When Sam first called out to them from the stage, microphone in hand, I just knew that he was going to kick us all out and tell Joe to find someone else to plan his events. But that didn't happen at all.

"Hey guys, do you want to listen to me sound check?" he asked the boys. "Why don't you sit down and tell me how I sound?"

Jason and Jonathan looked at each other, shrugged, and then stepped out of their skates and walked over to the front row of seats and sat down right next to Sam. For the rest of Sam's sound check, they offered a series of thumbs-ups and head nods when he asked whether there was any feedback, or if they could hear the bass along with the other instruments. It's a moment that the boys have never forgotten either, because, to this day, they refuse to go to a concert if they don't have the same level of VIP treatment.

Between Nashville Event Space and Hospitality Consultants, there was always so much going on, and more than ever, Allen was just as involved. He was on-site at aVenue most days to work with the sales team. On the days of events, he stopped by to make sure everything was executed perfectly. There were *lots* of events—around 250 or 300 a year, between all of our venues. We'd plan four on a typical Saturday, but during special events like the CMAs, there could be as many as ten in the span of one night.

By early 2007, Allen decided that it was time for him to leave Prudential and come and help me continue to build the company. There was so much money to be made planning events in Nashville, even more so as the city began to become more attractive to tourists and new residents. I was really good at what I did, and we had such a unique position in the market. In business, there is always a best time to launch and a best time to grow, and Allen knew that for Hospitality Consultants and Nashville Event Space, that moment was now.

At the same time, leaving Prudential would also give Allen the time to continue working as a financial planner by building his own portfolio of clients. He was great at what he did as well, and he had full intentions to continue to pursue his own career goals, even as we aggressively worked to take full advantage of the opportunities that were before us as event planners.

Allen wanted to capitalize on our unique business model, but he also wanted to become one of the most respected wealth advisors in the Nashville area.

Thankfully, he had the opportunity to do both.

CHAPTER 9

Beginning the year I turned thirty-five, I had gotten a mammogram done every June, typically some time close to my birthday. There is no incidence of breast cancer in my family, but I have always taken heed to the doctor's warnings about early detection and planning to have the screening done at the same time every year typically ensures that I won't forget.

By the time I turned forty-five, I was a mammogram pro. I'd never had a scare or any reason to be nervous; I simply showed up, got my healthy report, and reported back the following year. But that year, in 2007, I missed my appointment. aVenue was still growing, and I was so busy with Hospitality Consultants that I just kept rescheduling and rescheduling again. Before I knew it, it was February 2008. I was a full eight months late.

I wasn't surprised when my doctor told me she'd found a lump in my breast. I'd already felt it myself weeks before while watching TV on the couch with Allen. I knew enough to be concerned—if nothing else, the medical establishment has done a fantastic job telling women how dangerous lumps in their breasts can be—but I wasn't in a panic. At least not yet. Until that year, I'd been faithful in my checkups and explicitly following doctor's orders, so never once did I believe that I'd get cancer the very first time I missed an appointment.

After a mammogram, you are ushered into a room where you

are to await the results. If all is well, the doctor comes in and smiles and tells you to get dressed, that she'll see you in a year—same time, same place. Immediately, when my doctor came in and told me that I needed to have an ultrasound done, I knew something was wrong. There was a bright spot, however: the doctor who would be conducting the ultrasound was the mother of one of Jason's friends, and when she heard that I was the patient, she agreed to do it the same day.

Hours later, after more waiting and more tests, there was still more bad news. The doctor told me that I likely had breast cancer and that she would have to do a biopsy to confirm. Again, because she knew me through our sons, she agreed to do it immediately, even though it could be days before the results came in. Finally, I was told that I could get dressed and go home.

I was afraid, and I was emotionally exhausted, and I felt, in that moment, that my life would never be the same. As soon as I got to the car, I called Allen. I was crying hysterically when I told him that I might have cancer, that I might not live to see the boys grow up. I remember shaking uncontrollably and wishing that he was there with me, that I could feel his arms wrap around me as he told me that everything would be fine. I was so hysterical that I couldn't even put the keys in the ignition.

For so long I sat in the car, immovable, with the phone pressed against my ear as Allen whispered that everything would, in fact, be okay. He reminded me about the failed IVF treatments, Jonathan's surgery, and everything else we'd ever been through as a family. He reminded me all the things that we stared down and conquered even though we were scared out of our minds.

"We will beat this too," Allen said. "I promise."

That night, we decided to go out to a Chinese restaurant for dinner. I'd calmed down by then, and Allen and I had had a long talk about what was at stake, about what it meant that I potentially had this life-altering disease. At the same time, we decided to wait until we had the results before we talked to the kids. As parents, we wanted to protect our children from pain and trauma while also preparing them for the world, but without any definitive information, we thought it was best to say nothing.

We were still at dinner when the call came in. It was Dr. Tischler, a good friend of the family who also happened to be the head of the radiology department at Baptist Hospital. He'd reviewed my biopsy and, instead of waiting until the next morning, decided to call me that night with the news.

"I'm so sorry," he said, "but you have breast cancer."

———————

There is never a good time to get a breast cancer diagnosis, but that time certainly felt like the worst time.

With business doing so well and our family settled and thriving, we had recently moved to Franklin, Tennessee. While we liked the Bellevue area, Jason was going into middle school, and we wanted to live in a county with a great public school system. We focused our search in Williamson County and spent months scouring homes in Brentwood, about ten miles south of Nashville; Spring Hill, located on the southern border of the county; and even Leiper's Fork, which was further west and a bit more rural.

We wanted a home with office space and, ideally, a separate entryway. Being able to work and be home with the kids was very important to me, but I didn't want my employees to disrupt the rest of the family as they were coming in and out. Most importantly, we didn't want to build.

Allen and I looked all over the place, ultimately falling in love with Franklin and, specifically, a community called Timberline. It was an established neighborhood with lots of trees and green space as well as other families with small children. There were older families too, so we knew we wouldn't really outgrow the area. Unfortunately, everyone else seemed to love Timberline too, because there were never any homes for sale. We kept coming back, every other week or so, and there was just nothing. Then, one day, as we were heading back home after driving around in Franklin for what seemed like the hundredth time, Allen looked at me and said, "You know what? We should go through Timberline one more time."

I rolled my eyes and mumbled to myself that there was never, ever anything to buy there, but I smiled at Allen anyway and said, "Okay."

Lo and behold, as we were driving through, someone was literally in the process of putting down a for-sale sign in a plot of land that Allen and I had always assumed was the shared yard space of the two houses on either side. It was all grown in and there were benches there; in no way shape or form did it seem like this was a future home site.

We stopped and talked to the gentleman putting the "For Sale" sign in the ground and asked him, without even getting out of the car to look at the property, how much he wanted for it. He told us that he was selling the property for $99,000 and that he needed to have it all, in cash, by the end of the year for tax purposes.

We were excited but also realistic. It was late November/early December, so there wasn't much time to get the money together, and Allen and I weren't liquid enough at the time to cover the cost ourselves. Thankfully, when I called my sister and told her about the perfect property we'd found in the perfect neighborhood for our family, she agreed to give us the loan. Within a day, the sellers had the money.

It took nearly a year to build the house, but it was perfect. We had floors from Brazil; we had a custom deck in the back of the house; and we had enough space for seven of our twelve full-time staffers to work in our basement. Business was going great and only getting better.

Then came cancer.

———

From the beginning, I wanted to be as aggressive as possible in fighting it because I wanted to give myself the greatest chance of being around for the kids. I didn't want to risk the cancer returning or having to rely on a lumpectomy to get it all removed. Perhaps more importantly, I didn't want to become just another woman in Allen's life who had succumbed to cancer. He'd already lost his grandmother, mother, and sister, and I didn't want him to lose me too.

In retrospect, I can't imagine what Allen was going through, or how it must have felt for him to have to stand by while I endured such difficulties. Still, he held it together, and he agreed that we should attack this cancer with everything we had. Allen may have been falling apart on the inside, but outside, he was my rock. With his blessing, I had a double mastectomy on March 14, 2008, and a couple weeks later, I started chemo.

I was on a three-week cycle that was slated to last for seven months. I'd have treatment the first week and feel like absolute shit. The second week, I'd start to feel better and, hopefully, be able to go back to work by Wednesday or so. The third week would be the closest to "normal," and after that, I'd start back over from the beginning. This I was prepared to do, over and over, until the fall.

I was only one week into the first round of chemo when I began to seriously re-evaluate . . . well, everything. My only focus was on getting healthy, but at the same time, I had half-a-dozen employees working out of my basement daily and trying to keep my company afloat. I was extremely grateful that Allen had already stepped down from his position at Prudential and was able to take over the reins in my absence, but I just didn't feel like it was worth the effort. All I wanted to do was get better and raise my babies. I didn't care about CMA parties and artist meet-and-greets.

On a Wednesday morning, I had Laurie, who designed events and helped to manage some of the bigger accounts, come up from the basement into my bedroom to talk to me. Aside from Allen, she was, essentially, my right hand.

"I can't do this anymore," I said. "I'm going to have to close the company."

Breast cancer aside, Laurie had worked with me long enough to know that I was rather impulsive, that, sometimes, my emotions led me to decisions that weren't always in my best interests.

"Please, Randi, don't close the business," she said. "Let us handle it. We will take care of everything."

I trusted Laurie completely, so I told her that she had my blessing to take control and do what needed to be done. Her leadership gave me the freedom to get back to the business of fighting breast cancer, and years later, I would recognize that Laurie was one of the first angels sent to help guide me through one of the most difficult periods of my life. She would not, however, be the last.

———

Ask any cancer survivor and they'll likely tell you that, aside from the actual diagnosis, the moment when they begin losing their hair from the chemotherapy treatments is often the most difficult part of the process. Indeed, seeing chunks of hair come out in your brush served as a moment of reckoning: it is the moment when you can see—really see—how much your body has betrayed you, how much things will never be the same.

Like all things in my life, I decided that I wanted to lose my hair on my terms, and I decided to get the kids involved. We all went out on the back deck—me, Allen, and the boys. Then, I draped a towel around myself and handed Jason the clippers. "Here, guys," I said, "make Mommy bald."

They each took turns shaving swaths of my hair and they laughed the whole time, so tickled were they that their mom was going to have a head slick and shiny like a bowling ball. And while they laughed, I cried. I cried the entire time.

About a week later, Allen and I were shopping at a highly recommended wig shop in Goodlettsville. The shop sold wigs made of natural hair that were much more realistic looking than the synthetic ones on the market, but that didn't make the shopping experience any less traumatic. There was more crying, of course. It seemed like during that time, all I did was cry. Up and down the aisles, each time I passed another wig designed to hide the ugliness of my reality, I shed a few more tears.

"Honey, is this your first time getting a wig?"

I turned and looked in the direction of the voice and saw a woman sitting in a chair near the front of the shop. She had just picked out a wig and was getting it styled by the store's owner, while her husband slept in another chair nearby.

"Yes," I said through even more tears. "This is my first time."

The woman sighed and smiled, and she told me how she'd survived no less than seven different cancers. She'd had anal, brain, lung, and breast cancer, and there she was, full of joy and encouragement. "You're gonna be fine," she told me. "You're gonna get a great wig, and you're gonna look like yourself again. Pretty soon you're gonna feel like yourself again too."

She paused and then, with a glint in her eye, she added, "And be sure to watch for the angels along the way."

We talked for a few more minutes before the woman, now finished having her wig styled, got up to leave. My heart was filled with so much hope after having spoken with her, and I wanted to tell her how much I appreciated her, how much her words had already meant.

I was just a few steps behind her when she left the shop; the door didn't even have time to close behind her before I grabbed the handle and flung it back open again. I expected her to be there, perhaps a few yards in front of me, but when I looked, the woman and her husband were gone.

I took a deep breath and tried to calm the thoughts that were racing through my brain. I took another breath and looked to the right, up and down the street. I looked to the left. I looked everywhere and all around; still, there was no trace of them anywhere.

They had vanished completely, like angels called back up to heaven.

When I was given my diagnosis in February 2008, it was stage II breast cancer. Later, my doctor told me that the amount of detectable cancer was so small, so seemingly insignificant, that, had I made my appointment in June 2007, it may not have been detectable. At the same time, waiting just a few months later until my next appointment may have provided the necessary time for the cancer to grow and expand and be far less manageable than it was.

I always found it odd that I had developed breast cancer without any family history of the disease, but, more than anything, I was grateful to be healthy and alive. Years later, when a friend of mine who also had no history of the disease in her family also developed breast cancer, my perspective changed. My friend had recently had twins that she'd conceived via in vitro fertilization, and I had begun to make a possible connection between her cancer and the hormone treatments she'd taken.

In the years since, numerous reports and studies have been published that make a more plausible connection between the two, so I asked my oncologist about any potential link. While she wouldn't confirm it, she also wouldn't deny it. To this day, I am convinced that my breast cancer was related to my in vitro treatments. After all, before Allen and I made the decision to adopt, I had been through two rounds of in vitro.

It is estimated that one in eight American women will develop breast cancer at some point during their lifetime. Meanwhile, every single year, a quarter of a million women receive their heartbreaking diagnosis while more than forty-two thousand women end up dying from the disease. It is a sobering reality that should infuriate all of us who live in this country that has yet to discover a cure for breast cancer. But what infuriates me even more is the idea that so many women could be putting their futures in jeopardy without even realizing it.

A study published in *Annals of Surgical Oncology*[1] found that, among 3,375 women who'd undergone IVF treatment, 35 were diagnosed with breast cancer. This number was higher than the 24.8 cases that were expected based on breast cancer rates among the average population, leading the scientists to conclude that there is a possible association between IVF therapy and breast cancer development, especially among women aged 40 and over.

This study doesn't provide conclusive evidence for a link; neither have other studies conducted since then. And I understand that, for many women who are desperate to have a child, the risk of potentially developing breast cancer as a result of IVF, however minimal, may actually be worth it. The problem is that every year around four million American births are attributable to IVF, and those mothers aren't being told there's any risk at all.

This is what bothers me; this is the key detail that remains so prominent twelve years after I have been declared cancer-free. Yet it is also, in the grand scheme of things, a minor detail. More than anything else, I am grateful to be alive.

---

[1] I. Pappo et al., "The Possible Association between IVF and Breast Cancer Incidence," *Annals of Surgical Oncology* 15, no. 4 (April 2008), https://pubmed.ncbi.nlm.nih.gov/18214616/.

CHAPTER 10

I t's not an exaggeration to say that having—and surviving—breast
cancer completely changed my life. I think most survivors would
agree to this sentiment, even if we all have a different path to
recovery and a different way of viewing our post-cancer lives.

For many survivors, their recovery becomes the new foundation for the rest of their lives. They donate money to nonprofits
and participate in walks and 5k runs; they speak on panels and
volunteer for local charitable organizations. Their entire lives, it
seems, are consumed by cancer, even if the disease is no longer
ravaging their bodies. This commitment is understandable, of
course. It's a terrible disease and one that I truly hope we can find
a cure for one day. There is nothing more tragic than to see a life
cut short by cancer, or the lives left broken in its wake.

Still, even after I received my clean bill of health from my oncologist, I knew I wouldn't be diving head-first into cancer aware-
ness work. The work of organizations like the Leukemia and
Lymphoma Society and Susan G. Komen matters, of course, but I
knew that if I joined those efforts, I would lose myself in the process. And I didn't want to do that. I didn't want to be constantly
reminded of having cancer nor did I want people to know me only
as Randi Lesnick, *breast cancer survivor.* I just wanted to be Randi
Lesnick, the woman with a new lease on life and a second chance
to achieve her wildest dreams.

I threw myself back into my work, and thanks to Allen, Laurie, and the rest of my staff, there was actually work for me to come back to. They'd let me be sick when I needed to be sick, and when I wasn't sick anymore, they welcomed me with open arms and an overflowing events calendar. I will always be indebted to them for the way they ran the company in my absence.

While I was battling cancer, Allen kept everything under control and authentic to my initial vision for the company, so it was only natural that I brought him on as the official vice president of the company. We'd long been partners—he'd already been responsible for the company's marketing and finances—but this move made the partnership more official, even if only to the outside world. I also think it was a great way for me to tangibly express my profound appreciation and gratitude for him.

When Allen and I got married, we got married for a lifetime. We were both committed to loving each other through life's ups and downs, through rich times and poor, sickness and health, and all of the other vows that are traditionally shared at weddings. Still, I don't know that Allen anticipated that there would be so much sickness on my part. Even before breast cancer, I'd had a hip replacement in 2005, and Allen, as always, was right by my side, nursing me back to health and taking care of every single thing that I couldn't. And I was there for him too, bringing him meals in bed while he recovered from his own hip surgery years later.

Then there was the cancer itself, threatening to take me away like it took his mother, his sister, and his grandmother. I know that he was so overjoyed for me to beat it because he was my husband and he loved me more than anything, but I also think that he was happy that, if only this one time, cancer didn't win. We did.

I think about those days, when I was sick with chemo, with no hair, and I wonder if Allen was overwhelmed or tired or frightened. I know he was taking his meds every day, so I never worried about that. And he was always taking care of me, always there. He cooked; if I had a migraine, he made sure the drapes were drawn and laid in the bed next to me and rubbed my back until I fell asleep.

In the end, I think that, ultimately, he was just a natural caregiver. He was built for it. He was built for me, to love and care for me, and I think he was happy to care for me because he understood that I was up for the fight of my life against breast cancer. He knew that I was scared, and that I worried whether the treatments would work and whether the cancer would come back, if not in my breast, then somewhere else. So, I think he was happy to care for me and take everything off my plate so I could focus on the battle I was fighting. He wanted me to win just as much I wanted to—as much as our kids *needed* me to. And if he was overwhelmed or tired or frightened, he never showed it.

Allen was there for me years after breast cancer too, when I had my spleen removed and later when there was an ulcer in my colon. Now, when I think about the struggles that Allen was facing with his own depression, how that darkness was kept somewhat at bay by medication but was never fully lifted, I wonder if I should have done something differently, if I could have considered his feelings more. But there was just always something going on—with the kids, with the business, with my own health—and it was just easier to focus on those things. I didn't have time to consider Allen's feelings or his ability to cope with all of the turmoil every time it reared its ugly head in our lives. I was just grateful that he was there, grateful that God had given me my own Rock of Gibraltar that I could rely on completely.

That he could take care of me physically and emotionally while also helping to grow my business was more than I could have ever even hoped for.

———

In the period right after my breast cancer treatment, Nashville Event Space was incredibly popular and bringing in new clients on a daily basis, and because my staff was managing it so well, I could focus all of my energy on the music business. Like the group of the same name, Nashville really is a "little big town" where everyone seems to know everyone else, and word of mouth is often a far better advertisement than an expensive website or a highway billboard.

By 2009, I was easily the go-to event planner for all of Music Row, and not just because I was good at my job planning parties for many of Nashville's VIPs. For the most part, I was the only one doing it. For an industry that is filled with celebrities and relies on confidentiality as much as excellence, having someone who they can trust to plan amazing events without fawning all over the industry's biggest stars is very important, and I met both qualifications.

That's not to say that I wasn't always impressed by the constant pinch-me moments I was having while working as an event planner. I remember getting the call to do the party for the release of Ashley Michaels's third album, *Once in a Lifetime.* Ashley and Paul Christensen, who, by that time, had launched Music and Songs Records, Ashley's record label, wanted to have the event in New York, at the United Nations building. Everything was all planned and flights were booked for everyone who was flying in town, but then, three days before the event, the press corps had a meeting and decided to pull the plug. Apparently, word had leaked that Ashley Michaels was going to be at the United Nations headquarters for her album release party, and suddenly, the organization was bombarded with calls from tween girls who wanted to know what time they needed to show up so they could meet Ashley.

We had three days to find another venue to host this massive event; meanwhile, Ashley was in London, so she wasn't there to help us decide or make the final approval for the space. We had to move, and we had to move *quickly.*

I spent countless hours on the phone, scrambling late into the evening and calling all around town until I was finally able to talk to someone from an event venue called The Metropolitan. I was so excited that they agreed to let us host Ashley's event—often, in the world of event planning, locking down the venue is half the battle—and I couldn't wait to tell her about it.

Paul and I got on the phone to London to tell Ashley that we had the perfect place reserved for her and that she didn't have to worry about it all the way in Europe. But there was one minor detail that Paul and I didn't mention: we told her that we booked The Metropolitan, which was true, but Ashley believed that we'd booked The Metropolitan Museum of Art. Needless to say, we didn't correct her.

In the end, the event was beautiful; there were shimmering lights, pink and purple accents to match the album cover, and the letters from the words "Once in a Lifetime" carved into ice. Everything was just perfect. In fact, when Ashley arrived, she didn't mention anything about being miles away from the actual Met. Instead, she walked over to kiss the ice sculpture before kissing me on the cheek and saying, "Oh my god, Randi, this is exactly what I wanted."

There were other events too. There was the ACM Awards that I traveled to Las Vegas to host and the CMA events, sometimes ten in one night, that my company was in charge of executing. And there were countless weddings and corporate events, all adding to the bottom line and helping the company become bigger than I had ever imagined during that birthday party in 1998 when I dared to call myself a party planner and proceeded to harass the new head of Red Robin Records until he gave me the opportunity to prove it.

I was so proud of the work that I was doing and the business that I had built, but it wasn't the celebrities that I met, the house we were able to buy, or the extra zeroes on our bank statement that excited me the most. It was that fact that, alongside Allen, I knew that my mother was my biggest fan and that I made *her* proud every day.

———

Everything about me—the most important things, at least—comes from my mom. My drive, my work ethic, my ability to drown out the noise and work tirelessly to reach a goal . . . all of that, I learned from her. And I didn't learn it because she sat me down one day with a textbook and a highlighter and drilled the lessons into my head, one by one. I learned because I watched her, and as I watched, she broke through so many of the barriers that women faced in the 1970s and became a self-made millionaire.

She wasn't just working for the money. The money was certainly part of it, of course, because after she discovered that my father had been cheating on her, she wanted to become independently wealthy so that she never had to be taken care of by another man. But more than earning lots of money, my mother legitimately wanted to take care of her clients, and in the process, the money came.

The way my mother built travel packages that she knew her clients would enjoy and priced them at rates that were fair taught me everything I needed to know about building my own client-based business. And as my company grew, I looked forward to sharing every milestone with her, to asking questions along the way and continuing to build something we could both be proud of.

And that's just how it went—for a while, at least. Then, in 2011, I lost my biggest inspiration and favorite mentor.

CHAPTER 11

I was blessed to spend the last years of my mother's life right by her side, but the truth was, she never wanted to move to Nashville.

She made the move in 2001, after her husband, Larry, reached out and asked me to find a plot of land that they could build a house on. Allen and I were already well settled into our Franklin house by then—we'd already gotten to know all our neighbors and had fallen in love with the community—and I was able to find a property just a few miles from our house that would perfect for my mom and Larry's forever house.

We told her how much space she'd have, how she'd get to sit on her porch and walk around her yard, maybe even plant a garden—all stuff that she'd never been able to do in New York. And, of course, she'd get to spend more time with Jason and Jonathan as they grew up. My mom loved her grandkids, of course, but she wasn't remotely interested in leaving the only home she'd even known and traveling one thousand miles to the South.

It was bad enough that she was no longer working or growing the business that she'd built with her bare hands. My mother had already retired and was spending her days visiting my sister, Robin, and her children in Short Hills, and enjoying the fruit of her years of labor. She was so incredibly successful, with more money in the bank than she could ever spend, and I think she was looking forward to relaxing and spending the rest of her days in New Jersey. But thanks to her husband, she would be moving away to a land she had never known.

I didn't realize until later that my stepfather had pushed my mother to move because he wanted me to entertain and care for her as she aged. I only knew that she came kicking and screaming, that despite her love for me and Allen and the boys, my mother felt that moving to Tennessee was the worst thing that could have happened to her.

So, I kept her busy. We went shopping and had coffee in the early mornings at her kitchen table. She hung out with her grandkids, and she and Larry joined Old Natchez Country Club. That was where she spent most of her time when she wasn't at Jonathan's hockey games or watching Jason play the baritone in the Franklin High School marching band. Most important—at least for me—were the hours that my mother and I spent talking about business.

For so long, I had watched my mother from afar. When I was still a kid and Robin and I were eating dinner at the neighborhood diner while my mother built her company, I was fascinated by her ingenuity and resourcefulness, how she made something out of nothing and was able to provide an incredible life for us all on her own. Later, when I was older, and forgoing college to launch my own career, I looked to her for more practical guidance on how to achieve a level of success that matched hers.

By the time she arrived in Tennessee, my business was thriving, and I was excited to show her my achievements and make her proud. I took her to events with me and watched as she beamed with pride as I introduced her to the celebrities who trusted me to turn the most important moments of their lives into fabulous celebrations. When she couldn't go to the events with me, I called her as soon as I got in the car, relaying everything that happened and how much I wished she'd been there.

On the surface, the event-planning business was nothing like the travel industry. After all, my mother had spent her days on the phone with airlines and island resorts while I negotiated with caterers and furniture rental companies. Still, deep down, there were many similarities. To be successful, my mother and I both had to learn how to differentiate ourselves from the competition. We had to learn how to price our offerings to maximize both profit and client loyalty. And we had to learn how to provide customer service that was so great, our clients wouldn't even consider going over to the competition—even if the competition was cheaper.

When my mother and I talked about my business soon after she had moved to Tennessee, our conversations were like that of a mentor with a mentee. She didn't fully understand the world of event planning, but she knew enough about entrepreneurship to offer advice that I treasured and implemented fully. But soon, after she had been in Tennessee for a few years, I noticed that our relationship was changing. My mother was still so proud of me, and she wanted nothing but the best for me in my career, but I think she understood that I had reached a level of success that was perhaps beyond her realm of understanding. It was no longer me who was looking up to my mother as the embodiment of women's empowerment and entrepreneurship. Now, my mother looked up to me.

She would call Robin and my aunt Joan back in New Jersey and brag about all the amazing things I was doing, all the celebrities I was meeting. She would get so excited about going shopping with me when I needed to find a new dress for some awards show or after party that I was producing. And before long, I didn't even have time to call her afterward before my phone was already ringing, her voice high-pitched and anxious on the other end, begging me to tell her all about it.

Even now, I wish these moments could have gone on forever, but in the back of my mind, I knew that they wouldn't.

There is never a good time for your mother to get sick—to be diagnosed with lung cancer and begin the slow, torturous path to the end of her life—but it is most certainly not a good time when you are still recovering from your own bout with cancer, your body is still healing from the pokes and prods and countless rounds of chemo.

Allen and I later laughed about how, shortly after returning home from a treatment, Allen and Robin offered to go grocery shopping and asked if my mother would stay with me while I recovered.

"Sure," my mother said, "but can she make me a tuna fish sandwich?"

I was sitting in a chair in my room next to my mother, and all at once, everyone's eyes turned toward me. We all knew that my mother loved my tuna, that I knew how to put just the right amount of mayo in it for her very particular tastes.

My mother loved me, of course, and she wanted me to be able to rest and recover from my cancer battle. But she also wanted a tuna sandwich. In her way, I think that asking me for the sandwich was her way of saying that she believed I was fully healed and that she didn't see me as some sickly woman anymore, even though at that moment, I was fighting nausea and slipping in and out of a fitful sleep.

Allen and I laughed about it because this was just my mother's way, her strong, determined demeanor, the characteristics that I would adopt as I found my own place in the world. Then, a few months later, we found out that my mother was facing something that she wouldn't be able to beat or outsmart or will into submission. Then, we were crying.

My mother lived two years after her 2009 diagnosis before finally succumbing to lung cancer. The disease ravaged her body, and, for the last seven or eight months, she was confined to a bed that we wheeled out into the sunroom on the back of her house so that she could get some fresh air each day. All of us—me, my sister, Allen, and the boys—took turns sitting with her and stroking her hands; we talked to her and told her stories even when she was far beyond the point of being able to respond to us. And each day I would visit, I left her house with my heart torn to shreds—not just because my mother was dying but because so much of our world had been turned upside down.

When we discovered that my mother was terminal, I had personally taken her to meet with an attorney to ensure that all of her estate affairs were in order. She signed papers that dictated that everything that she'd worked so hard for would remain in her family, with my children and my sister's children.

I had already heard some disturbing stories about my stepfather's behavior. Friends mentioned that they saw him constantly returning clothes and other items that she'd purchased with her own money, and my mother's live-in housekeeper pulled me aside one day and told me that my stepfather had forced himself onto her. I knew how hard my mother had worked to build her fortune to the point that she no longer had to be dependent on a man, and I knew she wouldn't want her fortune to be left to a man who probably didn't have her best interests in mind. But that's exactly what happened.

Despite my advice to my mother that she shouldn't tell her husband that she'd changed the beneficiaries to her estate, she did tell him. The very next day, my stepfather took her back to that same attorney and had everything reversed and put in his name.

Once we came to fully understand what was happening to my mother, Allen took it particularly hard. On top of being frustrated that his kids would probably never see the inheritance that my mom wanted them to have, he couldn't understand why my stepfather had chosen someone else to handle my mother's investments when Allen and my brother-in-law Robert managed financial portfolios for a living. More than anything, though, Allen struggled because, at the same time my mother was losing her battle with cancer, his aunt was losing hers as well.

———————

Allen's aunt Maha lived in New York, and although she was not the aunt who took him and his sister in following their mother's death and their father's remarriage to a woman who was not interested in raising someone else's children, this aunt loved Allen like she was his own. Even after Allen was grown and married and had his own children, Maha checked in on him, making sure that he had everything he needed and that he wasn't letting the ugliness of his past impact the beauty of his present. Maha also treated me like I was her daughter, showering me with love and many pieces of jewelry from her personal collection.

Maha was Allen's father's sister, and she had seen the falling out between Allen and his father, Raymond, from up close. She saw how Raymond turned all his attention to his wife and her children from a previous relationship. She also saw how Raymond's massive collection of priceless art was being picked apart by his stepchildren. When Raymond told Maha that his stepchildren were taking pieces from his home without his permission, she thought about Allen and the Picasso that Raymond had promised him years before. And she took it.

Maha foresaw what would eventually happen once her brother died. Indeed, Allen received none of the inheritance from his father to which he was entitled. And if Maha hadn't already given him that Picasso, every single piece of Raymond's estate would have gone to his stepchildren.

As a result, Allen remained very close to his aunt, and he was devastated when she got sick, when she also died within a few months of my mother's passing in 2011. It was a very dark period for our family—dark and seemingly unchanging, at least for a while—but, as always, Allen served as the strong tower for our whole family, keeping us focused on all our blessings and helping us to look forward to brighter days ahead.

CHAPTER 12

By the fall of 2014, business was doing so well, and our staff growing so much, that the makeshift office in my basement was bursting at the seams. Everyone was packed so tight— sales reps and designers and marketing people. They were all sitting just inches from each other, their client calls bleeding from one phone into another due to the lack of privacy.

I wish I could say that I'd planned for this moment, that I'd forecasted business growth and hiring trends and had already sketched out a contingency plan for when we outgrew my home. But that's just not the case. The "just say yes and see what happens" spirit that had given me the courage to announce myself as an event planner back in 1998 without an ounce of experience was pretty much the same energy that I used to run the business. Allen brought much needed structure and strategy (with a heavy dose of skepticism), but I just always believed things would work themselves out on their own.

In September, I was designing a movie premiere for Reese Witherspoon at the Belcourt Theater in Green Hills. *The Good Lie* depicts the harrowing journey of a group of Sudanese siblings who are orphaned when their parents are killed by government militia and then find refuge in Kansas. Reese played Carrie Davis, an employment counselor who helps the Sudanese family restart their lives in America. Reese is also a Nashville native, so she wanted to host a premiere in her hometown.

I was driving to the event with Julia, one of my designers at the time, when we drove through Music Row and passed a "For Rent" sign that was situated in front of a tiny blue house situated between two bigger homes. As soon as we saw the sign, Julia grabbed my arm excitedly and pointed. She didn't have to say a word for me to understand what she meant: we needed a new office space, and there was nothing that said "top event planner of the country music industry" like having an office on Music Row.

As important as it is to understand how critical Music Row is to the country music industry, it's also important to understand just how coveted its real estate is. The growth of Music Row followed closely behind the growth of country music, which has consistently been one of the most popular music genres in America and certainly one of the highest revenue generators. By 2000, all the houses along 16th and 17th Avenues South (also known around town as Music Square East and Music Square West, respectively) were filled with the staffs of labels, publishers, recording studios, licensing companies, and a host of other companies related to country music. Indeed, Music Row was—and is—the center of the country music world. And here was an empty house, right in the center of the Row.

"Are you gonna call?" Julia asked, her eyes wide with excitement.

"I don't know," I said, shrugging.

The country music industry had always been a large part of my business—in fact, it was literally the foundation of my business, the reason why I went into business in the first place—but the truth was, I had never imagined working directly on the Row. I just assumed that we would work from my home in Williamson County, that I would only drive to Music Row for meetings and events. But now we had outgrown my home and, in a plot twist that I could have never scripted myself, there appeared to be space available for us on Music Row. I just wasn't sure if it made sense to make the move.

"Put the number in your phone, and I'll think about it," I said finally. "Right now, let's just focus on the event."

Minutes later, we pulled up in front of the Belcourt and started unloading. I was looking forward to the event and reminiscing about an earlier movie premiere that I'd planned, back in 2006, for Sam Thomas's *From Here to There*. The *From Here to There* premiere had been particularly special because it also marked the first time I was featured in the press as the main story and not just the designer of some event that was the actual focus of the piece.

During setup for Sam's event, a local publication stopped by to do a feature story on me and how I'd built a business planning events for some of the biggest names in country music. The reporter asked several questions about my business—why I decided to launch an event-planning business, how I got connected to the country music industry, a list of some of my favorite events that I'd designed over the last decade and a half. I answered all of the questions and smiled politely . . . until the reporter told me that he needed to take a picture of me to run alongside the story. To be clear, I didn't have a problem with being photographed. The problem was that he told me that I had to take the photo with Sam Thomas, who was standing nearby.

From the moment I launched my career and dove headfirst into the world of Nashville celebrity, I have made it a point to never ask for an autograph or a picture or lock of hair that I would later press between the pages of my diary. My stance on famous people is that they're, ultimately, still people, and I have always believed that if I had the chance to meet someone famous and eventually get to know them, the value of that interaction is in the relationship I formed with that person—not any memorabilia that I would hang in my house or want to sell on eBay.

As it turned out, Sam was close enough that he could hear the exchange between the reporter and me. He could hear me hesitate and say that if the story was about me, the photo should be of me alone, that if he so desperately needed Sam in the picture, maybe he didn't need a picture at all.

The reporter was flustered but still begging; then, out of the corner of my eye, I saw Sam making his way toward us in his signature cowboy hat.

"C'mon, Randi," he said, wrapping an arm around my waist. "All the years that I've known you, you've never asked for anything. Let me just do this for you."

"You don't have to," I said. "It's fine. Really. I know you're busy—"

Sam waved a hand to shush me. "I'm not busy at all. Now, let's take the picture."

Ten minutes later, the interview was over, and the reporter had his picture.

I thought about that as Julia and I were putting the finishing touches on the setup for Reese's premiere. I felt proud of what I'd accomplished, and I was thrilled by what was to come.

"Maybe I should call," I said, suddenly.

Julia didn't even look up from the linen she was stretching across two-top bar table. "Call who?" she said. Then, before I could respond, she lifted her eyes to mine.

"Oh, the house!" She started clapping while I laughed and reached for my cell phone.

Julia gave me the number that was printed on the sign, but before I dialed it, I called Allen. I told him about the house, where it was located, and how I thought it would be the perfect place for Hospitality Consultants to enter into its next stage of growth. I waited, expecting Allen to tell me to be more reasonable, perhaps more economical, but to my surprise, he said the opposite.

"Randi," he told me, "if there's a house available on Music Row, you need to take it."

Thrilled, I hung up the phone and called the realtor. I explained who I was, what my business did, and that I was interested in viewing the available property on Music Row. As it turned out, the realtor had just stopped by to check on the house and collect the mail. She said she was happy to stick around for a bit if I wanted to take a look that day, and she asked how quickly I could get there. With only a few minor details to attend to for the event—and nearly two hours before it would actually start—I told her I could be there in twenty minutes.

As Julia and I drove back to the house, I already felt as though something was shifting, as if, after seventeen years, I had finally, actually made it. I was already working in the industry so much, but now, everyone who was anyone would see my sign outside our office, either on their way to work in the morning or when they were driving back home at the end of the day.

The realtor gave us a tour, and during the entire walkthrough, I couldn't stop thinking about how beautiful the house was and, more important, how perfect it was for my business. Afterward, the realtor stepped away, leaving Julia and me alone. We were giddy like schoolgirls, talking through a plan for where everyone would sit, how we would decorate the office, and where we would hang our sign outside.

When the realtor came back in and asked if I was interested in the house, I didn't hesitate. I knew that the house wouldn't be available for long, that some upstart label or management company would see this prime piece of real estate in the prime location and jump on it if I didn't pull the trigger first. Most of all, I thought about Allen and how, if he didn't object, it was most certainly the right thing to do. A week later, I signed a year-long lease.

When I look back at the massive success that came to my business in 2015, I can't accurately attribute all of it to the move to Music Row, but the geographical move certainly coincided with a significant economic move for the company. We had never really had a bad year in the business before then, but we'd also never had a year as good as that one. On top of planning all sorts of events, from label holiday parties to weddings and corporate conferences, the calendar for the following year was filling up like crazy.

But even in the middle of all of that, there was something else to attend to. Like it had before, my health suddenly took center stage.

———————

If breast cancer taught me nothing else, it made very clear the value of health screenings and other preventative measures, so I made sure to get every checkup that was recommended by my doctor, including regular colonoscopies.

When I went for my colonoscopy in 2015, I already knew that I had a slight issue, that my doctor was not only checking for polyps or other abnormalities in my colon, but that he was also monitoring a situation on my nearby pancreas. There was a mass that had been there for several years and with every colonoscopy he was watching and waiting. This time, in 2015, he decided that we couldn't wait anymore.

"I'm sorry," my doctor said to Allen and me, "but I think you're going to need to go ahead and have this removed."

Once my doctor said "removed," the very next word that flashed in my mind was one of the most detestable words in the English language, the word that had most recently stolen my mother's life and Allen's aunt's life and had threatened to steal my own: cancer.

Immediately, Allen and I went into full research mode. If I was going to have this surgery done, we weren't going to cut any corners. We were going to find the best surgeon in the country, even if it meant leaving Nashville, even if it meant spending weeks away from home the way we did when we learned that Jonathan was at the risk of going blind. Ultimately, I asked my breast surgeon where she would have the procedure done if she were in my position, and she said, without hesitation, Massachusetts General.

I called and spoke to a doctor at Mass General; then we sent along all my tests results and copies of the CDs that showed all my scans so he could get a full picture, quite literally, of my current situation. Once he'd reviewed everything, he called me and said that he agreed with my doctor, that I definitely needed to have the mass removed and tested.

Time has a way of dulling the sharp pains of the past, making moments that once seemed unbearable feel, years later, like minor nuisances. For this reason, it is hard to verbalize the anxiety that Allen and I both felt in the weeks between learning that I needed to have surgery and then having the mass removed and tested for cancer. I remember feeling as though I was driving through a fog—I had no sense of how far I'd come or how far I had left to go before reaching my destination. All I could do was brace myself for an impact that may or may not come from something I couldn't see and wasn't really sure existed.

Allen and I flew to Boston on a Thursday and checked into a hotel. By noon the next day, I was being wheeled into the operating room and praying for a miracle.

I stayed in the hospital for a whole week while the questions remained unanswered and my future—with Allen, with my kids, with my business—hung in the air like a giant question mark. My sister came and visited, and she sat by my bed, clutching my hand as I tried to focus on the soap operas playing on the tiny TV hanging from the ceiling in the corner of the room. And there was Allen, smiling and strong throughout. I know now that he was just as worried as I was, the pessimist within him was only kept out of reach because he didn't want to scare me more. His role was to protect me at all costs—physically, emotionally—and he was committed to that role, even if it meant pushing his own fears to the side.

Finally, seven days after my surgery, the tests results came back. I didn't have cancer. I breathed a deep sigh of relief when the news came, and it was only then that I saw the burden that Allen had been carrying. Only when I saw the heaviness lift from his shoulders did I realized it had been there all along.

CHAPTER 13

Once Allen and I got the news that the mass on my pancreas wasn't cancerous, we were finally able to take a deep breath. There was still a road to recovery stretching out far in front of me, and I still had to be cleared before we would even be able to travel back home to Nashville. Still, each of those things seemed like minor inconveniences once we learned that I didn't have cancer again, that I wouldn't be forced through endless rounds of chemo again, forced to fill my body with poison and watch it kill the healthiest parts of me even as it worked to destroy the awful invader.

The boys were both in school—Jason at University of Tennessee-Knoxville and Jonathan at Limestone College in Gaffney, South Carolina—so, as we waited for clearance, Allen and I decided to make the most of our time in Boston. It's a beautiful city, with its old-world charm and modern sensibilities, and we enjoyed exploring as much of it as we could. I spent much of the day sleeping while Allen worked. He checked in on his finance clients as well as our employees at aVenue and Hospitality Consultants; once again, I was blown away by how well they were able to keep everything moving in my absence. My battle with breast cancer may have been the catalyst that pushed my team to find their own sense of leadership and accountability, but by 2015, they were a well-oiled machine, easily holding the company together in my absence.

In Boston, Allen and I stayed in a hotel near the North Bank Pedestrian Bridge and in the evenings, after I'd slept and Allen had worked, we would venture out. I was moving slowly, of course, trying to get some exercise and wake up sleepy muscles, but Allen was there, his arm linked in mine, keeping my footing steady. We would get food and talk and just be grateful that, finally, all the struggles we'd faced seemed to be behind us. Indeed, when we finally made it back to Nashville, we didn't just discover that things had continued on without us. We discovered that things were positioned to be better than ever.

As the winter of 2015 settled over Nashville, we already knew that we were in for a huge year in 2016. The lead time on events is quite long—a year, most often—so the best way to forecast a year's earnings is to look at the previous year's books. All throughout 2015, including the time I spent in Massachusetts, the phone continued to ring. Corporate events, weddings, music industry functions . . . You name it and it was on our calendar, filling it up until it was overflowing.

Suddenly, we discovered that we had to hire and train more people, that we weren't fully equipped to handle the amount of business we were bringing in. It was a welcome problem to have, though, as well as a lovely confirmation that all of Allen's efforts to design aVenue's website and move the company into the digital age had been worth it.

We also had to find another office space to accommodate our rapidly expanding crew. We were nearing the end of our lease at our first Music Row space when, in November of 2015, just a few months before our lease was set to end at our current place, Allen found another property that was just up the street. The house at 1601 17th Avenue South was big and airy with its own parking lot out back. The front yard was wide and the staircase that led to the front door was intercepted by a large porch that was perfect for kicking back, having a drink, and watching all of our music industry neighbors. I immediately fell in love when I saw it, and instead of renting the new house, Allen and I decided to buy it.

Typically, I would have to beg Allen to make a decision like this, convincing him that the money spent would return to us in spades. This time, however, I didn't have to. I'm sure he crunched the numbers and drafted his own growth model to estimate the increase in equity we'd receive over the coming years. But more than anything, the fact that the address of the house was 1601 and we were moving into 2016—a year that would be the biggest in the history of our business—felt like a wink from God. The purchase felt like a calculated investment as opposed to a dangerous risk, and now we weren't just visitors to the Row. We had planted roots and were there to stay.

In the end, 2016 was a whirlwind like nothing we'd ever seen in the history of Hospitality Consultants. I remember standing in awe of it all, how the little company I'd thrown together at the spur of a kid's-birthday-party moment was on track to gross $5 million in annual revenue. My company and my success as an entrepreneur was proof that you could win as a woman in business, that you could overcome personal and family tragedy and keep going, and that you didn't have to resort to sleazy sales tactics to get customers. Word of mouth was my primary system for new clients leads in 1998, and even seventeen years later, nothing had changed.

I remember looking at Allen in the early summer months of 2016, smiling wide, and saying, "Can you believe it? Can you believe how well the company is doing? It's just amazing, isn't it?"

Allen smiled politely but he definitely wasn't as excited as I was. "Yes, it's great," he said, "but I'm worried."

This admission was no shock to me. Allen was always worried about something—it was his nature, after all—and I'd learned to accept it and move on. Sometimes his worry was helpful, as his pessimism forced us to be overly prepared for the future, but most of the time it just hung heavy like a storm cloud, threatening to ruin even the sunniest day. As far as I was concerned, we were having the time of our lives, we had the bank account to show for it, and there was absolutely nothing to worry about.

"What's wrong now?" I said, rolling my eyes.

"Nothing's *wrong*," Allen said, his voice tinged with frustration. "I'm just thinking about 2017. We should have gotten more bookings by now if 2017 is going to be anywhere near as successful as this year."

I nodded. I understood his logic, and it was his job to handle the numbers of the business. But even though I respected his practical concern, I had to defer to my own optimism.

"It'll be fine, Allen," I said, wrapping my arms around him. "Everything always works itself out."

I leaned my head against his chest and felt it heave as he sighed. "I don't know, Randi. I just don't know."

Well, Allen was right about 2017. It was a good year, but it wasn't as good as 2016. Not even close. We had to do more on social media and on the website, and we had to deal with the fact that our business model was no longer as unique as it had once been. Now, as venues had witnessed how much money I made by having them sign exclusive contracts and requiring them to use me for all events, they began hiring their own planners in an effort to keep any revenue generated from events in house.

I think we had expected that day to eventually come—if nothing else, Allen certainly did. But as it turned out, the biggest issue we faced in 2017 wasn't the number of events we booked or the challenge of bringing new venues into the Nashville Event Planning leg of our business. It was, once again, my health.

———

One of the perks of having a healthy business was that I could engage in acts of self-care without thinking twice about the expense, and one of my favorite ways to relax has always been massages. Every Monday night for years, I had a massage therapist come to my house and give me a massage in the privacy of my bedroom. And on a Monday night in late spring, I asked her about a lump that had been growing on my left side, just adjacent to my abdomen.

"Do you feel that?" I asked her, motioning in the direction of the lump.

I felt her fingers root around, soft but gentle, until they stopped suddenly. "Yeah," she said, "I do."

When I told her that it had been there for a few days, I saw concern sweep over her face. I'd already suspected that the lump signaled something bad, but I'd also grown so tired of doctor's offices and hospital operating rooms. I didn't want to be sick again, and I didn't want to have to put my life—and Allen's life—on hold once again.

I'd been wrestling with uncertainty about what to do next, but the nudging from my massage therapist was the final push I needed.

"I would check it out if I were you," she said, "just to be safe."

I nodded and thought about my bout with breast cancer, how I'd been saved as much by medicine as the timing of my checkup. I'd gotten diagnosed just late enough that the cancer was detectable, but also early enough that it was still stage II and highly treatable.

The next morning, I called my doctor's office to see when I could come in to have the mass looked at. My appointment was scheduled for Friday, and in the days between, I tried to keep my thoughts trained on best-case scenarios. I assumed that I was experiencing an attack from diverticulitis, a condition that is triggered when bulging pouches on the intestines become inflamed or infected. I'd had diverticulitis for years at that point, so I was familiar with the symptoms that could occur . . . but that still didn't explain the lump growing from my abdomen. That had never happened before.

By Thursday night, I no longer had to think about it anymore. I was so sick with delirium, I was vomiting nonstop, and I had a sky-high fever. Allen told me to grab my things and we headed straight to the emergency room at St. Thomas Hospital.

I can't remember how long we waited—I was woozy and my head was spinning—but I do remember what happened when the doctor who'd evaluated me delivered his sobering news.

"You're not gonna make it to Monday if you don't have surgery. This lump is in your colon. It's caused by diverticulitis, and it's going to kill you if you don't take care of it. You need to have your whole colon removed, immediately."

My first thought was not about my health or even the concerns of Allen, who was sitting right next to me with his head in his hands, his heart undoubtedly wracked with fear once again. All I could think about was what would happen if I had my colon removed.

"So, I'll have to wear a colostomy bag for the rest of my life?" I asked the doctor.

"Yes," he said, flatly. "That is an unfortunate side effect of this life-saving procedure."

His words only confirmed what I already knew, and as I narrowed my eyes and pulled my body upright on the narrow hospital bed, I said, "Well, then, I'd rather die."

"I don't think you understand," the doctor said, unable to mask his surprise. "This is not something you can live with for months or even weeks. I'm telling you that your body will start shutting down quite rapidly and you won't last longer than a few days."

The last statement was all Allen needed to hear. He jumped from his seat beside the bed and, with his eyes welling with tears, asked the doctor if he could have a minute to speak to me alone.

For the next hour or so, as the doctor filled out paperwork to have me admitted to the hospital and I was taken to my new room, Allen pleaded with me to have the surgery. He didn't have to tell me that he was scared. I could hear it in his voice and see it in his body language, how he sat hunched over, wringing his hands constantly. He loved me and wanted to spend the rest of his life with me, and there I was, upset about having to wear a colostomy bag.

We spent the weekend in the hospital. Most of the time I was sitting sprawled across the bathroom floor with my head pointed inside the toilet while nurses worked around the clock to manage my symptoms as much as they could. And all the while, Allen was holding my hand, silently begging me to have the procedure.

I wish I could say that it was Allen's pleading that caused me to change my mind, that I was considerate of his feelings and the reality of his future without me. I wish I had decided immediately to have the surgery, for his sake and our sons'. But it wasn't until Monday morning when the doctor returned and told me that I'd run out of time, that this was the last moment to save myself, that I had my final revelation. I didn't want to die.

I wanted to live.

CHAPTER 14

I awoke from surgery at St. Thomas groggy and foggy-brained. As my eyes adjusted to the fluorescent light from above and my mind started to clear, I began to piece together the days that had passed—the sickness that had swept over my body and how close I had come to death. As I squinted my eyes against the brightness, I assumed that I was on the other side, that I had escaped death. But I wasn't sure.

I slowly lifted each finger of both hands as they lay down by my sides, then I wriggled my toes and let my eyes scan the room around me. It was as if I was the star in a movie about a woman who'd been in a terrible accident and woke up suddenly in a hospital bed, afraid she'd been paralyzed. I had decided that I wanted to live, but I was still aware that this might not have been possible, that I may have taken my last breath on the operating room table. I wanted to be sure that I was still alive. I wanted confirmation that God had given me yet another opportunity to exist.

Of course, Allen's face was the first thing I saw as I looked around the small room. He was sitting in a chair pushed next to a window, and I couldn't help but notice how he'd aged. Allen was sixty-one then, having lived a whole lifetime since we'd first met in New York in 1988. I'd been with him the whole time—day after day, month after month, year after year. But it seemed as though, in that moment, I was seeing him for the first time in a long time.

The creases around his mouth looked a little deeper, the skin around his eyes a little puffier. He was aging, as we all do, but a dull throbbing in my gut told me that I was to blame.

When Allen finally noticed me staring at him, his eyes grew wet with tears and his lips parted into a smile. A wide smile. I knew that he was just as happy as I was that I had made it out of surgery alive, but there seemed to be something else driving his happiness.

"I have something to tell you," he told me.

The first time I tried to speak, my voice cracked and came out barely above a whisper. I stopped, took a sip of water from the small pink pitcher on the table next to my bed, and tried again. "What is it?"

"I know you were worried about having to wear a colostomy bag—"

I lifted a hand to cut him off. Deciding to have the surgery was one thing but getting comfortable carrying around a sack filled with fecal matter for the rest of my life was something entirely different. I didn't want to think about it. I definitely didn't want to talk about that.

"Not right now," I told Allen. "I just got out of surgery. Can we please have this conversation later?"

"I think you're going to want to hear this," Allen said, smiling again.

I sat silently for a moment tried to read his expression. "Fine," I said. "Tell me."

"I talked to the doctor while you were still in surgery. He told me that they only had to remove six inches of your colon—so, just the infected part."

"Okaaaaay," I said, slowly. "I still don't understand what that means."

"It means," Allen said, "that you still have most of your colon. And because you still have most of your colon, you don't have to wear the colostomy bag forever. You'll have it for six months, but in December, the doctors will be able to reverse it."

I had no words for the relief that swelled in my stomach and rose up through my chest, so I just lay my head back on my pillow and sighed. Finally, I felt alive.

The relief from surviving surgery and learning about the colostomy bag reversal was short-lived. Before I was discharged from the hospital, I learned that my glucose levels were extremely high. Because I'd had my spleen and a piece of my pancreas removed, my body was no longer producing enough insulin to direct the glucose in my bloodstream into the cells where it was most needed. Instead, the sugar was lingering in my bloodstream, poised to trigger a slew of complications, from nerve and kidney damage to cardiovascular disease.

I was given explicit instructions on how to manage the disease with the hope that, like the colostomy bag that would temporarily close the six-inch gap in my colon, my diabetes could be reversed as well. I was told to avoid foods that were high in sugar as well as foods that would ultimately turn to sugar inside my body. This included bread and grains and even excess fruit.

A friend of mine, Diane, had always been really into health and nutrition, so once I got home from St. Thomas, she was the first call that I made. Not only was I unable to cook due to my recovery, but I honestly didn't know how to cook in a way that wouldn't exacerbate my sickness even more. Diane dropped off bags of produce from the farmer's market and made delicious salads and sheet trays full of roasted vegetables to go along with baked fish or poultry. There was no red meat on the menu, no wine or other alcohol either.

But no matter how much I stuck to the new diet, I still had to have daily insulin shots—at least until we could get my diabetes under control. And in those early days, when I was still bedridden, covered in bandages, and loopy on pain medication, that responsibility fell entirely on Allen. He learned how to gently roll the bottle of insulin between his hands to mix the medicine together. He learned how to thrust the needle into the insulin bottle and pull the back until the exact number of insulin units that I needed were drawn in. And he learned how to pinch the fat of my stomach or thigh and hold the needle at a forty-five-degree angle, pushing it in quickly and cleanly to give my body the nutrients that would keep it healthy and alive.

This, in itself, would have been a manageable load. Allen could have given me my two shots of day, finishing each round in less than five minutes once he got really efficient. But it wasn't just that. I needed help with everything then, including changing the colostomy bag that was affixed to my abdomen.

For the first couple weeks, I had a nurse who would come to the house during the day. She would check on me and make sure everything was healing as it was supposed to, and, of course, she would change the colostomy bag and clean around the incision before reattaching a new one. Because of this, those early days were relatively tensionless between Allen and me. He changed my bag at night, once the nurse had left for the day, and in those first two weeks, he did it with care and understanding. He was happy to care for me then when everything was still new and the joy around my very existence was still fresh.

But I was going to have to wear the bag for six months—a whole half-a-year—and what started out as a necessary and justifiable task that Allen was happy to endure soon became a burden that he was still willing to bear, but grudgingly.

Even without Allen's frustration from the day-to-day drudgery of caring for me, I was already beginning to feel my own emotional challenges. I had always been independent, fiercely so, and I hated that, once again, I suddenly wasn't. I'd gone from being bedridden with breast cancer, to spending weeks at a hospital in Boston to have a mass removed from pancreas, to defecating in a plastic bag after an emergency, life-saving surgery. And I hated every moment of it.

I wanted to be the Randi that traveled the country for work, bouncing from Alaska to Florida and everywhere in between. I wanted to be the Randi that later traveled the world with my husband, exploring vineyards in Italy and islands in the Caribbean. I wanted to throw myself into my business again, taking it to heights unseen, exploring new opportunities and defeating new challenges. I wanted to do anything but be an invalid who depended on Allen for every single little thing. On top of that, I know that Allen wanted the same thing.

He was still caring, still loving, but he was tired. On the surface, I think he was tired of the bag changes, the trips to the kitchen to get me water and food, plus the running of the business mostly by himself as I spent long days and longer nights huddled beneath my covers. But I also think he was just tired in general. I think he was tired of me being sick, not because it meant that he had to take care of me (even though it did mean that), but because it meant that I was always on the verge of leaving him.

My breast cancer was stage II, so if I didn't survive, it would have been a longer, slower road to death. We would have had time to adequately prepare and say our goodbyes. But this time, with this illness, everything happened so fast. There was no time to plan or think, only frightening moments of him imagining life without me. Then, when I made it out alive, he was rewarded with the task of nursing me back to health, even though he'd never had time to care for his own battered heart.

I needed Allen to give me my shots, to change my bag, and to help me take a bath. With each new time that I told him I needed something else, his eyes grew tighter, his shoulders more tense. It aggravated me that he was aggravated, but, again, I was so focused on getting back to myself that I couldn't see that he felt that he was losing himself.

After a few months, once I was healed enough to move around on my own and the diet changes had started to reverse my diabetes diagnosis, I learned how to change my colostomy bag myself. I wanted to be independent again, but I also wanted to make things easier for Allen. I had never seen him so distraught, and it scared me.

In addition to relieving Allen of some of the load he was carrying, doing more on my own also helped me to feel a lot better about myself. Slowly but surely, I was starting to break out of my funk and get back into life as a wife, mom, and business owner. I started checking in with my team more regularly; then I started having calls with clients again and doing more strategic planning. By November—still a month before I was to have my colostomy bag reversed—I was able to help my team plan ten separate parties for the Country Music Association's annual awards show. The night of the CMA's is known annually as "Country's Biggest Night," and it felt so good to be a part of it. I was back in my element, back doing what I loved with the people I loved doing it with.

By the time New Year's Eve rolled around, there was only hope in the forecast for the next twelve months. With the most traumatic experience of my life behind me, I felt like anything was possible. Surely there wouldn't be another health scare. Surely there wouldn't be another reason for Allen or me to be nervous about what the next day might bring.

All of that was behind us, and as we looked ahead to 2018—my twentieth year in business—we knew that nothing was going to get in our way.

CHAPTER 15

E very year, as the calendar turns from December to January, we know that the earliest part of the year will be the slowest months of business. Aside from the stray New Year's Day wedding or the occasional Valentine's Day party, the event-planning business typically takes the first couple months of the year to take a deep breath after the holiday season, but before the busyness of spring kicks in. For Hospitality Consultants in the year 2018, January and February were also used as a time to plan for our twentieth-anniversary celebrations.

I was just six months removed from the surgery that ultimately saved my life, and just a few weeks beyond having my colostomy bag reversed. Needless to say, I was still a ball of emotions, still so grateful to have the opportunity to see the dawn of a new year. Every day felt like a gift; every moment spent with my boys and with Allen felt like a blessing that I couldn't have imagined while lying in the operating room just months before. There was already so much for me to be thankful for, even without considering that I was entering my twentieth year in business.

If life is simply a series of decisions—a bunch of yeses and a string of noes—the fact that my company had persevered for two decades was simply a testament to my willingness to continue to show up, to continue to follow the path that God had laid out before me. At the birthday party for Jason's friend in 1998, I saw an opportunity to transition to a new career and launch a new company, and I took it.

After that, when other record labels in town attended my events and decided that they wanted to work with me too, I followed that path and walked through those doors as they opened, even when it meant that I had to completely change my revenue model to accommodate them. Later, when I had an opportunity to manage venues instead of simply hosting my own events there, I said yes. I said yes while battling breast cancer, when my team begged me to keep the business alive, when they promised to keep everything afloat even as I felt like I was drowning. Then, around April of 2018, I said yes again when I received a call about a new project in Huntsville, Alabama.

I got a call from Dan and Patsy Yancy, who were operating a new mixed-use space called Stovehouse. Operating on the grounds of a former stove factory, Stovehouse featured restaurants and bars, retail, and office space. The Yancys also wanted to include a couple of venues for locals looking for a cool, new place to host their weddings and corporate gatherings, so they blocked off two spaces—one five thousand square feet and the other ten thousand—with the intent to upscale, "ultra-modern" venues. But unlike the restaurants and boutiques that were managed and operated by the owners who'd founded them, there was no one to run these planned venues and ensure that they became profitable. That's where I came in.

The event spaces were still under construction, but the Yancys wanted to find someone who could oversee that process and also manage the venues once they were ready to open. They asked around for suggestions and their architect—whom I'd never met—recommended my company, just one hundred miles away in Nashville.

Over a series of phone calls, the Yancys explained their vision for the two event spaces and how they believed that they would elevate the Stovehouse complex overall. I was immediately interested. We'd already done some venue management with aVenue, but this project would take everything I'd learned to a new level. It would also require me to expand my knowledge and skills even further. The Stovehouse project was more than me coming into an already established space and telling them how they could make some extra money; I would be involved from the very beginning, working directly with the Yancys to ensure that every decision made—from lighting to integrated technology and bathroom design—would have long-term benefits. It was an opportunity to help build two world-class venues from the bottom up.

Once I decided that I definitely wanted to work with the Yancys, a few members of my staff and I traveled to Huntsville to view the space. We toured Stovehouse, ate at a restaurant downtown, and got a good sense of the leisure destination that the Yancys were in the process of creating. Then we came back to Nashville to draw up a feasibility study.

The goal was to communicate, in a written report, how viable I believed the proposed venue spaces at Stovehouse could be. *Could they make money? How much? How soon?* Those were some of the questions I was supposed to answer in my report. In truth, I had never done a feasibility study before. I'd closed countless deals by simply building relationships and working incredibly hard to exceed expectations every time. That was still the strategy, so I came home, googled "feasibility study" and got to work producing a report that would not only convince the Yancys and their bank that their two new event spaces would, indeed, prove very profitable—but that I was the person to help ensure their success.

The Yancys accepted the study, and we prepared to embark on a long-term partnership that wouldn't fully commence until construction was complete. In the interim, I went back to planning in Nashville, but I was beginning to sense a shift in my desires and my approach to my career. I loved what I did, but I also longed for something more—a new challenge, a new opportunity, perhaps some way to share the lessons learned over years of experience with younger women who were trying to figure out how to have families and pursue their professional goals at the same time.

Perhaps it was the Stovehouse project that opened my eyes to all that was possible; all I knew was that I couldn't go back to the same daily routine that I'd lived for the prior twenty years.

Allen saw this too, and he supported me wholeheartedly. As the chief financial officer of the company, his job was to make sure that we kept revenues high and spending to a minimum, but he backed me when I decided to hire a publicist who was able to land a couple of features on me and my business, as well as a new staff member who was going to focus solely on increasing my social media platform. I wasn't quite sure how I was going to leverage that platform—maybe start doing paid speaking gigs or write a book—but I knew that if I wanted to have any level of influence in the era of Facebook, Twitter, and Instagram, I at least needed to have the platform built.

Finally, Allen and I decided to launch a whole new leg of the company called Venue Rescue. Like aVenue, which allowed us to expand on our current business model and pre-established skill sets by serving as a third-party events manager for venues, Venue Rescue would also help us expand on our core competencies. The call from the Yancys in Huntsville was proof that people respected my level of expertise, not just as an event planner but as a venue operator who could maximize profits. They wanted to work with me because they wanted to make more money and serve more people, and I quickly realized that the Yancys weren't the only businesspeople in that boat.

In the same way that Allen built the Randi Events website and optimized it so that people looking for "event planners in Nashville" or "Nashville wedding planner" would find us, he began building the Venue Rescue website to reach businesspeople like the Yancys. If there was an entrepreneur sitting on an empty space and wanting to know how to use it to host events and bring additional revenue, we wanted them to find us.

Meanwhile, as Allen and I continued working on ways to expand the business offerings of Hospitality Consultants/Randi Events, I began planning my twentieth-anniversary party. I wanted something grand and magical, something that accurately represented all the beauty and amazement I'd brought to all my clients over the years. More importantly, I wanted to recognize all the people who had helped me along the way. That included my team members, of course, and I reached out to many of them, including people who hadn't worked for me in years, and asked them to come and celebrate with me. It included my vendors, companies like Music City Tents and Events that were there with me from the beginning and made it possible for me to stay in business as long as I had. And it also included the many clients who made my company possible, who hired me year after year after year, even when they didn't have to, even when we didn't have an official contract.

If there was anyone at the top of the list of clients who made my work possible, it was Paul Christensen at Music and Songs Records.

My party was scheduled for September, but a few weeks before, I took Paul and the top executives at Music and Songs out to a special dinner at Kayne Prime, a boutique steakhouse in The Gulch. Paul and his team had a scheduling conflict that would prevent them from attending the anniversary event, but there was no way I could celebrate my twentieth year in business without showing my appreciation for Paul and the rest of his Music and Songs team.

I'd met Paul in 1998, when I planned that first event for Red Robin Records to celebrate their grand opening. We hit it off immediately, eventually becoming great friends, and when he left to start his own label, he took me with him. From Music and Songs's CMA events to album releases and number-one parties, Paul kept my number on speed dial. His faith and loyalty certainly provided a lucrative revenue for my company, but it also gave me the validation that I needed as I worked to establish myself as the go-to event planner for Music Row. Paul signed Ashley Michaels when no other label in town was interested, and as her stardom was rising, he trusted me to help bring her creative vision to life at all her events.

I was so grateful for Paul's belief in me as an entrepreneur and for our personal relationship, and I was so excited to show him my gratitude. During the dinner at Kayne Prime, I presented Paul with a special plaque that commemorated all the events I'd thrown for him over the past twenty years. It was such a special moment for me and my team, and it was the perfect pre-celebration leading up to the twentieth-anniversary party.

On the day of the party, I was extremely emotional the whole day. I was overwhelmed with joy and appreciation for the years passed, and I was filled with excitement and anticipation for the years to come. Everything about the event was perfect—from the food to the décor and the music—and I had such an incredible time celebrating with all the people who meant so much to me.

My son Jason came with his fiancée, and while he'd always known what I did for a living and had the opportunity to attend some of the events I'd planned, I think the anniversary party really illustrated the magnitude of the business his father and I had built. Neither of the boys had ever expressed any interest in working for the company or taking it over after Allen and I passed away, but I think that night may have changed things for Jason.

A few months later, in mid-December, Jason and his fiancée came over for dinner. They brought dessert and a plan: Jason had been working for Apple, but he wasn't happy with his position or the hours and was looking to do something else. His idea was to come and work for Randi Events, to support the marketing team and help expand the company's digital footprint.

I remember my heart swelling with pride and joy. I think it is the dream of all entrepreneurial parents that their children play a role in the family business, and I was overjoyed that Jason was finally doing just that. I was even more thrilled at how perfect his timing was. My social media manager, whom I'd only recently hired, had just put in her resignation notice, and told me she was leaving the company at the end of the year.

As we were thrown into the holiday rush of Christmas and New Year's Eve parties, I hadn't had time to think about replacing her, but there was my son, stepping up at just the right time. I grabbed his hand across the dinner table and told him that he didn't even have to ask, that he was always welcome in the company.

And I smiled. It was the perfect way to end an incredible year, and a wonderful sign that there were plenty more great things in store for the year to come.

CHAPTER 16

We're all busier than ever these days. We order our food from DoorDash and hire someone to scrub their floors; we skip our daily workouts and spend less time with the people who matter most. This a common concern amongst businesspeople especially, whether they're launching businesses or trying to grow them. And with it, there is a common refrain, a piece of go-to advice for those whose to-do lists contains more tasks than there are hours in the day: just say no.

Like the addict who is trying to break free or the teenager considering their very first hit, we are encouraged to say "no" to all the extra things that exist just beyond our current responsibilities. According to the experts, those are the things that throw us off-kilter, that jeopardize our relationships and our health and, ultimately, cause us regret.

While I understand this advice as someone who has always moved in a million different directions at a thousand miles an hour, I still struggle to embrace it for myself. In 2015, Shonda Rhimes published a book called *The Year of Yes* that was all about her saying yes to every opportunity that came her way over the course of a year. People flocked to this book, and it quickly hit the *New York Times* bestseller's list (Rhimes is, after all, the creator of *Grey's Anatomy* and several other hugely popular TV shows). But I couldn't help but wonder what all the fuss was about.

Shonda Rhimes may have had one year of yes, but I'd had a lifetime of yeses, and with each new year, I was always on the lookout for all the new ways I could say yes, yes, yes.

In 2019, that opportunity came early, when I received a call in January from a past colleague whom I hadn't talked to in more than thirty years.

———————

Mike and I worked together in Anchorage, Alaska, when he was a front office director for Hilton, and I was the director of sales and marketing. We became friends, and I even spent a weekend at Trail Lake Lodge with him and his wife, Sonja. We fished for halibut and king salmon, and we celebrated all that we'd achieved as business colleagues.

Mike respected my tenacity and willingness to work hard. There weren't many women around back then, but Mike never made me feel that I was out of place or that my insight wasn't valuable. In fact, when we talked about how we'd achieved 105 percent occupancy at a hotel all the way in Alaska, Mike always acknowledged my efforts as much as his own.

Eventually, Mike and I lost touch, as people often do. At the outset, we both stayed with the company, though I ultimately left after moving back to New York and refusing a transfer to Atlanta. That began my foray into consulting work, as well as my earliest stints in entrepreneurship and, of course, my introduction to Allen and the beginning of our lives together. Still, relationships with solid foundations have the ability to stand strong through the years—even when life takes both people in different directions.

When Mike sent me a message on Facebook—*Hey! It's a blast from the past!*—I was so excited to hear from him, and I immediately invited him out to visit Allen and me in Tennessee. It would be the perfect opportunity, I thought, for us to meet the other's spouse and catch up on what we were doing career-wise.

I didn't even mention that I'd launched my own multi-million-dollar event-planning company and had long before left the hotel business behind. I wanted to save that conversation for our first dinner together; I wanted to tell him in person how hard I'd worked to get my company off the ground and how proud I was that I'd kept the doors open for two decades. I didn't even realize that he'd already done his homework and knew exactly what I'd been up to.

A few weeks later, over plates of medium-well steaks and Caesar salads, Mike told me that he was working on a new project with Russell Hospitality in Atlanta. They were already managing a soul food restaurant called Paschal's, and like Stovehouse in Huntsville, they wanted to expand their offerings to include an event venue.

I nodded as he was explaining. Then, between bites of food, I asked him to tell me more about the space and what they were hoping to accomplish. At that point, the project in Huntsville was far from being completed, but Venue Rescue was well underway, and I was definitely eager to sign my first client.

I began mentally preparing my spiel, deciding how I would explain to Mike everything that I'd been doing for the past twenty years. But as it turned out, Mike had already googled me (first under my maiden name, Toltz) and learned all about Randi Events and Nashville Event Space. Thanks to Allen's insistence that we build two beautiful websites that fully showcased all we had to offer as an event-planning company and as managers of top event spaces, Mike had a general understanding of how I could help him well before he ever pulled his car into my driveway.

"Well," Mike said, "there's this adjoining space called The Loft that we're thinking about doing something with. It's just a big empty space right now, but we were thinking it may make for a great events space and could help bring in some additional revenue outside of the hotel and restaurant."

"Okay," I said, assuming he was going to ask me for some advice about how to bring this new plan to fruition. "Who do you have working on it with you?"

Mike took a sip of his red wine, eyeing me over the top of his glass all the while. "That's the thing," he said. "We're not working with anybody right now, but we were thinking that maybe you could do something with the space. Kind of like what you did with aVenue."

"Yeah," I blurted, without a second thought. "I'm sure I could help you guys out. I'd need to come check out the space, of course."

Mike grinned. "Of course, of course. I'd love to have you come down and take a look, tell me what you think. I know that the Russells would like to move pretty quickly on this, so do you think you could schedule some time in the next month or so?"

I didn't have to talk to Allen or even look at him to know how he would feel about this conversation, about my willingness to jump headfirst into something brand new. He would tell me to slow down, to take my time, to think things through before I make a verbal commitment.

But he also knew me. He knew that I wanted to move out of the day-to-day drudgery of negotiating contracts, planning events, and chasing payments to focus more on consulting. He knew that the business was essentially on autopilot, that we'd built a team who could keep things moving forward even if I was out doing something else. I trusted the girls who were working for me, and after twenty years, I was more than ready to jump in and try some new projects. It's what I'd always done, and it was how I'd built my business in the first place. Allen knew that too.

I took a sip of my own wine and returned Mike's smile. "Sure," I said. "Coming to Atlanta won't be a problem at all."

By the time Allen and I left for Atlanta to view the property, he was just as excited as I was about the new project. I loved the business that we'd built together, but it had been a long time since I was genuinely enthusiastic about the work we were doing. So much of it had become routine, and I think Allen saw that working with Mike and Russell Hospitality could be a new beginning for me as we waited for the venues at Stovehouse to be completed.

When we arrived in Atlanta, however, his opinion quickly shifted.

Allen's personality veered toward the negative, toward the glass half empty, and when he saw how outdated the space was, he immediately second-guessed our involvement. He couldn't see past the work that needed to be done; I, on the other hand, saw only minor issues that could be easily remedied. Sure, the walls needed to be repainted and the space needed new light fixtures. In the grand scheme of things, those were minimal expenses—and certainly nothing that would get in the way of the work I knew I was capable of doing.

I couldn't completely vouch for the venue, and my relationship with the Russells was too new for me to have a really good sense of what kind a partner they would be. But if nothing else, I knew that I was a hard worker; I knew that I could make something out of nothing; and I knew that I could turn a concrete box into a top event venue if I had to—and I could do it blindfolded with one hand tied behind my back.

But if there was any part of the process that I wasn't so sure about, it was drafting the proposal to secure the partnership. I was so eager to land the deal that I made big promises and, ultimately, overcommitted.

I pledged that, for the first three months, Allen and I would be traveling to Atlanta two days out of the week for meetings and planning purposes. Now, Nashville is only about 250 miles from Atlanta—a four-hour drive each way on a clear day with no traffic. Allen and I made the drive ourselves when we first went to look at the property, and I remember thinking that it wasn't so bad, that it wouldn't be a big deal to make that trip on a regular basis. But once a week, every week, was far from regular. It was excessive, and it quickly took a toll on Allen and me.

Back and forth, back and forth, back and forth. Each trip back and forth to Atlanta put just a little more pressure on Allen and me until it eventually felt like we had one hundred pounds of baggage strapped to our backs. At the same time, we were also arguing about the best way to execute the project overall.

At this point, Allen and I had been working together for over a decade, but I was the lead on the project, and, ultimately, I had a different opinion about how the job needed to be done. In the proposal, I clearly outlined how much Russell would have to spend for renovations if we were going to come on board. That wasn't a problem in itself—Allen definitely agreed that the venue needed work—but he didn't think I asked for enough money. I presented a number that I thought was fair and that would allow us to get the necessary renovations made without scaring off Russell Hospitality, but, from the very beginning, Allen questioned whether I would be able to do everything that needed to be done at the price I'd quoted, or in the amount of time I'd promised. I was sales and relationships, the negotiator who sealed the deal and secured the check. And Allen was the numbers guy, always pulling out his calculator to forecast and decide whether we were on track.

Thanks to his background in banquet sales, Allen was also the food and beverage guy whom Russell called on to provide suggestions on how to improve operations at Paschal's and the neighboring Clarion Hotel. The only problem was that Allen found the operations at Paschal's and that neighboring Clarion Hotel to be irredeemable.

When we stayed at the Clarion and went down for breakfast in the mornings, he would always complain that the food wasn't right, that the phone number on the website for the restaurant wasn't right, that the employees weren't doing their jobs well and properly representing the company. I understood his frustrations, but my role in the deal wasn't to focus on those things. I was tunnel-visioned on making sure the event space was a success, which, at the outset, meant undertaking a massive renovation.

In retrospect, I can see clearly that things were spiraling out of control, and it was happening very, very quickly. But in the moment, as we were bringing on a new client and working to ensure that the client was happy and that we were making money, I didn't think about the cost to my team, or to Allen specifically.

He'd always been so strong, and we'd always been able to get past so many challenges together. I assumed that this time would be no different, that after a few months, things would calm down and we'd settle into a more manageable groove.

I had no idea that the worst was still ahead.

CHAPTER 17

When Jason and his girlfriend got engaged in 2018, Allen and I were legitimately happy for them. More than anything else, I've always wanted for my kids to be happy, and if they were able to find someone who could make them happy, I was all for it. But I also knew that young love had its challenges.

Case in point: Just a couple months before the wedding—far past the date when most of the logistical details should have been squared away—Jason met with his fiancée and her mother, as well as one of my designers who was planning the wedding, to pick out the invitations. Allen and I decided to come too, but not because we wanted to hover over the soon-to-be-newlyweds or insert our unsolicited opinions.

As it stood, the invitations were set to mention the parents of the bride only, and Allen and I knew that if we wanted our family acknowledged, we would have to make sure it happened ourselves. So, we waited patiently and quietly for Jason and his fiancée to find the shape and design that best reflected their wedding theme; then I gently but forcefully remarked that we wanted the invitations to state that Mr. and Mrs. Allen Lesnick also wanted to be listed as extending the invitation to witness the joining of husband and wife, as well as two separate families.

In retrospect, we would have hoped that Jason would have

spoken up for us in our absence, but we couldn't depend on that, nor could we depend on his fiancée or her family to acknowledge us. Still, we didn't hold this apparent slight against Jason's fiancée. If anything, Allen and I knew that the early twenties are a time for learning and understanding the world around you, and for discovering your place within it. It can be challenging, then, to embark on a serious relationship when your very identity is still in flux. As a result, we also weren't terribly surprised when Jason told us that the wedding was off.

We were in Atlanta when we got the call, just finishing dinner in a downtown condo courtesy of the generosity of one of the girls on my staff. Her family had a house far out in the Georgia country, about an hour outside of Atlanta, so her parents also purchased a condo in the city. They were gracious enough to let Allen and I stay there whenever we were in town, giving us a bit of an at-home feeling, even when we were four hours from home and travel weary.

It was the Tuesday after the meeting with the invitation designer and just a few days after the cake testing when Jason called. So, when I saw his name flash across the screen of my cell phone, I assumed he wanted to talk about the wedding or, perhaps, the event he was bartending for that night. Then I heard his voice, and I knew something was terribly wrong.

"Mom," Jason said hysterically, "I need you and Dad to come and get me. Now."

"What do you mean come and get you?" I asked.

His words choked in his throat as he struggled to pull back his tears. "The wedding's off, Mom. I'm moving out, and I need you to come and get me so I can come back home."

I put Jason on speaker and set my cell in the middle of the table so Allen could hear Jason's response when I asked him to explain everything that had happened.

He told us that he had just gotten to the event when the first call came in from the invitation designer. She told Jason that his future mother-in-law had just called to cancel the invitations and he wanted to know if that was okay with him. Next came the call from someone at their wedding venue. The story was the same, that Jason's mother-in-law wanted to cancel the contract and the person on the other end of the phone wanted to make sure that he was aware before giving their reservation to someone else.

Jason told us that his mind was racing by that point, that when he tried to call his fiancée, he got no answer, just one ring after another until he was prompted to leave a message on her voicemail. But what would he say? *Hey, people keep telling me that you want to cancel the wedding, so can you call me back and let me know if it's true?* Hours later, Jason still hadn't spoken to his fiancée, but he had finally accepted the reality that his wedding wouldn't be happening after all.

As Jason was talking, I watched Allen's face crumple with anguish. Allen hurt for his son, of course. No parent wants to see or hear their child in such obvious distress. But I could see concern cloud his eyes; I could see that he was worried about how he and Jason would coexist in the same space for the first time in years. Allen and Jason's love for each other was never questioned, but like many parents and their adult children, they didn't always get along. Their personalities clashed like stripes and plaids, ripping and pulling on already raw nerves until there was nothing left but open wounds.

———

By the early summer months of 2019, Allen and I were traveling to Atlanta every Sunday and staying until Wednesday before heading to Nashville. It was a massive commitment—a sacrifice really—that chopped our weeks in half and forced us to reorganize our lives around the trips. On its own, the frequency of travel was already daunting, but Allen was also concerned that spending so much time away was going to hurt Randi Events, that we'd lost our focus and ability to prioritize. I, on the other hand, was laser-focused on expanding into new revenue streams.

It hadn't been long since we'd gotten the call from Paul Christensen that he'd received a too-good-to-ignore offer for the building where aVenue was housed. A company wanted to use the space to operate their bar and club in partnership with one of the hottest young acts in country music, with three levels for food and music and dancing. I told him that he had to take it, that he was sure to make far more money with this newest venture than he could with aVenue and that business was business.

So, while Paul moved and continued to expand his portfolio, it was up to me to fill the gaping hole aVenue left behind. It would be a while before Stovehouse in Huntsville would be ready to open, so The Loft in Atlanta seemed like the best option for diversifying our revenue streams as well as the type of work I was doing.

That's not to say that it would be an easy transition from 100 percent event planning to some mix of planning and consulting. Nothing is easy, certainly in the beginning. I knew this, and Allen did too; my collapse at my very first County Radio Seminar was the perfect illustration. So, I never expected that we wouldn't feel a little worn out and spread thin in those early days, and I didn't even expect us to make any money until our second year. But I knew that once we turned the corner—once we'd worked through the kinks and found our rhythm, just as we had with Hospitality Consultants and Randi Events—our efforts in Atlanta were sure to pay off.

With this in mind, I kept my head down at The Loft, working on the remodel and redesign while putting together a marketing strategy that would generate increased profits. We wanted to leverage the fact that The Loft was within walking distance from Mercedes-Benz Stadium where the NFL's Atlanta Falcons and Major League Soccer's Atlanta United team play. To cater to this discerning clientele, we suggested that The Loft offer more premium services, like valet parking, and we began to lead their team's social media and digital marketing efforts. We wanted to make it very clear that The Loft provided upscale experiences of the highest quality, and we knew that it was going to take some work to get Atlanta residents to believe that. Allen, meanwhile, was spending more and more time trying to improve things over at Paschal's. He was giving suggestions to the waitstaff, the bartenders, and the chefs too; he was laser-focused on creating a top-notch experience for all customers.

The owners, thrilled about the value we were adding, soon wanted to make adjustments to our agreement. They increased the monthly retainer they were paying me and agreed to reimburse us for expenses related to travel and room and board. They even encouraged Allen and me to fly between Nashville and Atlanta as much as possible.

Still, these concessions did nothing to relieve the exhaustion that Allen and I felt, or Allen's worry that we'd somehow miscalculated, that our focus on crossing every t and dotting every i in Atlanta would cause something to fall through the cracks in Nashville. The more involved we got in Atlanta, the more Allen worried that our balance was off, and even though there was no way we could have prevented the dissolution of Jason's engagement, his frantic phone call seemed like an astute confirmation of Allen's greatest fears.

After Allen and I hung up with Jason, we didn't hesitate to pack everything up and hit the road immediately. Within a couple hours, we were traveling north on I-75, connecting with I-24, and navigating the mountains near Chattanooga as we crossed the Georgia-Tennessee border. The next morning, we rose early and met Jonathan at Jason's place in Thompson's Station. He'd already packed clothes and personal belongings and we loaded everything in our cars before heading back to Franklin.

We knew that Jason would need time to regroup and start again, and as his mother, I was prepared to give him that. His heart was already broken, so I wanted to save him the stress of also having to find somewhere that he could live that he could afford on his own. Allen shared this sentiment, at least initially. But Allen was also concerned that Jason was almost thirty and had appeared to have lost his way, that more than feeling grateful that he could come back home, Jason, a grown man, seemed unwilling to defer to our authority again.

In retrospect, the contention around Jason's move back home was just one straw in a basketful that was beginning to weigh heavily on Allen. What's more, Allen was in no position to deal with any of them. I didn't know it at the time, but he'd recently stopped taking his meds. He was most certainly feeling better, the result of the warm summer sun and the prospect of new business conspiring to make him believe that all was well, that he didn't need to rely on pharmaceuticals in order to function.

But like a recovering alcoholic who would credit a year of sobriety to his body's inability to get drunk, instead of his abstinence from alcohol, Allen's decision to stop taking medication was completely ignorant of the reality of depression.

Depression is not an on-and-off-again thing that sometimes needs attention but can otherwise be left alone. It is, instead, a ravenous monster, always waiting for an opportunity to grow big and scary in the dark, always looking to devour its sleeping prey.

CHAPTER 18

We were back in Atlanta, a few weeks after the broken engagement, and I noticed that Allen wasn't acting like himself. His personality naturally veered toward the quiet and introspective, but this was different. He was keeping completely to himself, saying only a few words over coffee, not wanting to talk at all about the ongoing project at The Loft. In fact, during that four-day trip, he didn't even want to go into the Atlanta office with me. He told me that he had some client business to check on—he was still maintaining his wealth management practice—but I suspected that there was something more at play, that he simply wanted to be alone.

At the same time, progress was marching forward with The Loft. We'd already put up new chandeliers and drapes in preparation for the upcoming grand re-opening, and we'd scheduled two weeks of painting to begin on September 9. After many back-and-forths with the owners, I'd finally convinced them that they needed to be willing to spend a considerable amount if they ever hoped to make any in return. My philosophy was that I could walk into any event venue and tell the owners how they could make the space profitable, but the caveat was that the space itself had to meet profit-worthy standards.

Needless to say, I was busy. Too busy, I think, to give Allen the attention he deserved during those four days when his health started to take its final, most terrifying turn. I kissed him goodbye each morning when I left for the office and called multiple times during the day to check in, but I couldn't be there with him. I wasn't there to see that he was barely eating, that instead of actually working on his client accounts he was spending the days staring out the windows of the condo or lying in bed with the covers pulled to his chin. By evening, when I returned, he would once again feign normalcy, pretending that he was fine, that he'd just needed to rest. And I would say okay, pushing the worry back to the furthest corners of my mind as I prepared myself to get up the next day and start all over again.

I did, however, suggest that Allen call Tom, his psychologist. Again, I had no idea that Allen was no longer taking his medication, I just knew that I wanted him to call Thom because we knew and trusted him. It was Thom whom we called shortly after we'd moved from New York to Nashville, when Allen had suddenly become overwhelmed with our new life with two kids and a new job in a strange town with no family nearby. And it was Thom who had been keeping Allen healthy ever since, scheduling regular sessions to talk him through his fears and concerns and making sure he had access to the necessary medication that would manually adjust the chemicals in his brain when Allen's body couldn't do it on its own.

Thom had become such a fixture in our lives that I just assumed he would always be there and that he would always keep Allen healthy. So, when Allen seemed to be beginning a slow spiral while we were in Atlanta—and while we were in the midst of a very important and very big business project—I naturally believed that Thom would fix it. He had the training and the knowledge to get to the root of Allen's issues in a way that I couldn't.

Normally, Allen drove us back to Nashville, but on that Wednesday, he was still so withdrawn, his eyes so expressionless but distanced, as if he were staring at something far away. I took the keys from him and slid into the driver's seat myself.

We were about an hour-and-a-half from home, driving past Tullahoma, when I reached out and placed a gentle hand on his.

"How did the call go with Thom?" I asked.

Allen turned his gaze to the passenger's side window as fields of vast green whizzed by. "It went fine," he said.

"Well," I said, feeling my stomach knot, "how are you feeling now?"

Several silent moments passed before Allen responded with another "fine"—a "fine" that I obviously didn't believe.

I peppered him with more questions: *What's wrong? Do you think you need to talk to someone else? Do you want me to take you to a hospital? Is there anything else I can do to help you?*

Over and over again he responded with one-word answers, if he responded at all. He was barely talking—barely breathing, it seemed—just a hollowed-out version of himself. I sighed and searched my brain for answers to the very questions I was asking, and still I came up with nothing. The atmosphere inside the car was heavy with uncertainty and apprehension, like the scene in a thriller movie just before the bad guy breaks in with a gun. Everyone in the theater is on edge, awaiting the final terror, though no one knows just how—or when—it will come.

At the first stoplight as we pulled into Murfreesboro, just south of Nashville, I pulled out my cell phone and sent a quick text to Jonathan and Jason:

Driving back from Atlanta, but something's wrong with Dad. Please meet me at the house. We'll be there in 45 minutes.

———

When we pulled up to our home, Allen didn't ask anything about Jonathan's car being there, parked right next to Jason's, even though it was much later in the day than when he normally visited.

I ushered him out of the car quickly, leaving our bags behind. I wanted to get him inside and sit him down so he could talk to me and the boys. I wanted to see if Jason and Jonathan saw what I did, if they would be as worried as I already was.

They were not.

An hour later, while Allen was in the bathroom, Jonathan put an arm around my shoulder and told me that he was leaving, that Dad seemed just fine to him. His words sent my stomach into my feet and made my heartbeat double-time, but I didn't tell him that. I didn't want him to be as scared as I was, and, more than that, I wanted him to be right. I wanted Allen to be *just fine*.

As Jonathan left and Jason retreated to his room in the basement, I looked at Allen, who'd returned from the bathroom and taken a seat next to me on the couch in the family room.

"Can you go outside and get our luggage from the car?" I asked him. "We didn't bring it in earlier."

Allen smiled and said, "Sure," and I continued to let myself believe the best-case scenario, that maybe he was just having a hard time being in Atlanta because he wanted to be at home. I decided to make a cup of tea, and as I poured the boiling water over the bag of chamomile, I searched my mind for an alternative.

No job, I was beginning to realize, was worth jeopardizing Allen's health. If the travel was too much for him, I could go back and forth by myself, maybe with a few of the girls from the Nashville office, and Allen could stay behind. It's what he would want, I decided as I heaped a teaspoon of honey into my mug. He could work from the Nashville office each day and make sure that everything was taken care of, that nothing was falling through the cracks like he feared.

I was already back on the coach, tea in one hand and TV remote in the other, when I realized it had been nearly twenty minutes since I'd asked Allen to go and get the luggage. *I must have missed him come back in*, I thought to myself as I got up and walked toward the other side of the house. The door of our home opened to a large entryway. To the left was the kitchen and family room, where I was sitting. To the right was my office and our bedroom.

It would have been totally possible for Allen to come in and go straight to our room without me noticing.

This is what I was thinking as I passed the front door and heard a strange sound coming from the driveway. I stopped, backed up, and opened the door to find Allen, bent at his waist behind our car with both palms planted firmly on the trunk.

He was screaming so loudly that I was sure the neighbors would hear, but it wasn't the words coming from his mouth that concerned me most. It was the sound coming from his body, the guttural howls that seemed to come from deep within. When I looked at the man leaning over our car, I saw someone who looked like Allen, my husband of nearly thirty years. But he wasn't Allen. He was someone else entirely.

I spun around, ran back into the house, and screamed for Jason to come up from the basement. Moments later, he and I were standing in the driveway with Allen, wrapping our arms around his waist and trying to pull him back inside the house. All the while, Allen was spouting crazy gibberish that made no sense, his body heaving up and down as if he had been holding his breath for hours and was fighting for air.

"I've lost all our money," he said. "I'm going to jail. I'm going to jail, Randi, and I've ruined everything! I'm so sorry! I'm so, so sorry!"

Fighting back tears, I told Jason that I needed to call for help, that there was no way we could help him on our own. Allen was having a psychotic breakdown, and I was afraid of what would happen next if I didn't call.

I didn't think that Allen was paying attention to me. He was so outside of himself, so out of control, that I didn't even think he could hear me. But he did. He heard every word I said, and when he heard me say that I was calling for help, he assumed that I was calling the police, that I had believed what he said about losing our money and was turning him in to the authorities.

In a blur, he broke free from our grasp and tried to run. Jason stood in front of the door, so he couldn't get back outside, but he was still acting wildly and panting madly as he tried to find an escape. I slipped away long enough to call 911; in the interim, all we could do was try to keep Allen from hurting himself. Keeping him calm, as the emergency operator suggested, was no longer an option.

Moments later, the police cars and ambulance arrived, sending sickening sirens echoing through our neighborhood, their vehicles blocking driveways and front yards all around. We had become a spectacle, but in that moment, my neighbors' judgement was the furthest thing from my mind. My husband was spiraling, and I didn't know if we'd ever be able to pull him back up again.

In the end, it took eight grown men to physically subdue Allen, to lay him prone on the ground so that they could sedate him, place him on a stretcher, and get him loaded into the back of the ambulance. While they did that, Jason called Jonathan and told him that there'd been an emergency and he needed to meet us at the hospital.

Once Allen was safely inside the ambulance, the paramedics clasped the double doors behind him, got back in their vehicles, and disappeared as quickly as they'd arrived. Meanwhile, Jason and I watched as they drove him away—my husband who'd always been so strong, now crumbling under the weight of his sorrow.

CHAPTER 19

O nce our street was completely cleared of emergency vehicles, I went back into the house to make sure the dogs were okay and grab my purse. Then Jason and I got in the car and headed toward the hospital.

I remember crying the whole way as my mind searched for an explanation. I wanted to know that this was a fluke, that Allen wasn't really as sick as he'd looked when he was flailing on the ground, all six feet, two inches of him resisting the emergency personnel who'd come to save Allen from himself. I needed to know that this was a hiccup, that he hadn't been this sick all along, that I hadn't stood blindly by as my beloved husband suffered. But as soon as we got to the hospital, I knew.

Allen was very, very sick. He was rambling and incoherent, bouncing from one topic to another, none of it making any sense. He told me that he was going to jail, that he lost all our money, that I was going to have to close the business. I had no idea what Allen was talking about, and every time he opened his mouth, I grew more and more frightened. I didn't know the man lying before me; I didn't recognize him at all.

Then the psychiatrist came out and told me that he needed to speak to me, that there was something important I needed to know about Allen's condition. I nodded as tears began to well in my eyes. The truth was, I couldn't take any more information.

Already, I'd watched my husband of nearly thirty years have a psychotic breakdown in our driveway, and I'd had to stand by as his son witnessed it. I was exhausted and heartbroken, my soul already carrying much more than I'd ever thought it could bear.

When the doctor told me that Allen admitted to going off his antidepressants in June, I immediately flashed back to the months after Jonathan came home, when I'd watched Allen get overwhelmed by his new reality. He wasn't taking his meds then either, so when life stepped in with two babies and a wife and a demanding career, he didn't have the tools to cope in a healthy way.

Then my mind went back. First, I rewound to June of that year, to the days when there was nothing but promise and possibility before us. We'd started 2019 on such a high note—I was healthy, we'd just celebrated our twentieth year in business, and we were both on the same page about diversifying our revenue streams through consulting work and other new projects.

Everything was great then, and I could understand how Allen got carried away by it all, seduced like a lonely man who falls prey to a smiling woman in a red dress. The earliest days of those illicit affairs are marked by exhilaration and optimism; only after the woman's husband returns from war does the poor man realize that he was never in control, that he was, instead, a victim of his extremely fickle emotions.

Then my mind rushed forward even further, and I considered everything that had been piled on Allen's plate in just the last few months. Already we were running a multi-million-dollar business while Allen maintained his roster of wealth management clients, and that was before Jason's broken engagement and the new project in Atlanta—two separate stressors that, standing alone, would have tested the limits of anyone's patience. So, I understood how Allen could have hit a wall. I understood how he could feel that the whole world was exploding all around him, and that he wasn't equipped to handle it all himself.

All told, I understood how Allen could have been deceived

enough by the early days of summer to stop taking his meds and believe that he was well enough to navigate life on his own—only to be reminded, just a few months later, of the cruelness of life.

Once I understood and could begin to see the magnitude of the issue we were facing, I became incredibly focused on the solution.

"How do we fix him?" I asked. "How do we get my husband back to normal?"

The psychiatrist nodded solemnly and pulled out his chart. "For starters, we're definitely going to need to admit your husband," he said. "He's not well, and right now, he's a danger to himself and to you."

"Yes, okay," I said. "I understand."

"Also," the doctor said, "we're going to need to increase his medication. He stopped taking it for three months, so we need to get his body reacclimated. I'm proposing a cocktail of sorts that will help readjust as quickly as possible."

I nodded again, even though I had no idea what a cocktail was, or what it meant that he was essentially proposing that my husband essentially take a double dosage of his previous antidepressant medication. All I knew was that I wanted Allen to get better.

Allen spent five days in the psych ward, and each day I sat with him from four to six p.m., until the duration of my timed visit was up, and I was forced to go home alone and sleep in a bed meant for two. Even if I thought that Allen was improving, the safety measures taken in Vanderbilt's psychiatric ward were evidence that my husband had a long road ahead of him. He wasn't allowed access to any shoelaces or belts; even my purse had to be locked up when I was there.

On Jonathan's birthday, the boys and I went to see Allen together. It was supposed to be a joyous occasion, a reason to celebrate, but all I could think about was how my sons must have felt to see their father in that state, in that drab room with no curtains or pencils, not even a TV remote. But we were family, and if the head of our family was suffering, we were going to be there to support him like he was always, *always* there for us.

Once Allen was discharged, we knew that the work was only just beginning. He'd been referred to another psychologist, and though he wouldn't have his first appointment for a full three weeks, thanks to an extensive waiting list, Allen was also required to attend group therapy sessions. Allen wasn't thrilled by this, of course. He had no desire to reveal his demons to complete strangers—strangers who were as sick as he was.

"It's actually good," I said, "because the therapist's office is right around the corner from our office. I can drop you off on my way to work, and I'll come and pick you up when you're done. Then we can go back home."

Allen's looked at me and looked away, his face devoid of emotion. "Okay," he said. "That sounds good."

When it was time for his appointment, I pulled up in front of the therapist's office and kissed Allen goodbye. I hated that I had to leave him there, alone, but I kept telling myself that something good would come from it. If it took a mental breakdown and a stint in the hospital for us to get Allen back on track so that he could spend the rest of his life healthy and whole, all of it would have been worth it.

As I drove off, I waved, and Allen waved back. He didn't look completely like his old self yet—his shoulders were still slumped, his eyes still dark and empty—but he looked hopeful and determined to finally beat this monster that had taken control of his mind. I didn't realize, however, that he had no intentions of going inside, that as soon as I pulled away from the curb he was going to walk across the street and spend the whole day at a pizza joint.

Had I known, I would have pushed back when he told me he wanted to drive himself to group therapy the next day. Had I known, I wouldn't have been so surprised when I received the phone call that he had been kicked out of the program.

"I'm sorry, Mrs. Lesnick, but this is the second day Allen hasn't showed up for therapy," the receptionist said.

I rushed to close the door to my office, trying to create some space between my husband's sickness and the rest of the office.

"I don't understand," I whispered into the phone. "I dropped him off myself on the first day. I pulled up right in front of the office, and I watched him walk right up to the front door."

"Mrs. Lesnick, I believe you." The woman's voice was laced with pity. "I'm just telling you that he never came inside, and because he never showed up for his scheduled session, he's going to have to be disqualified from our program."

"Wait, wait!" I said, frantically. "He just got out of the hospital, and he needs this therapy. Can't he have another chance?"

"I'm sorry, Mrs. Lesnick," the woman said, "but there are just too many people waiting to get into this program. We're going to have to give his spot to someone who is more committed."

———

Hours later, I was sitting at the kitchen table at home and googling group-therapy programs in Nashville when Allen walked through the front door, disheveled and disheartened. He looked like he'd spent the day literally running from his demons.

We were supposed to have dinner that night with friends we hadn't seen in months. We were close to this other couple, and not just because we tried to get together regularly for food and drinks and a good time. These friends had also watched our kids grow up, and they'd been there through my battle with breast cancer and all my surgeries. Still, despite our deep bond, I didn't feel comfortable telling them what Allen was going through. I couldn't tell them that I was scared out of my mind and unable to work, to eat, to sleep.

As Allen drug himself into our bedroom to shower, I called our friends and told them that we weren't going to be make it.

"Allen just got out of the hospital," I said. "He was severely de-hydrated but he's doing fine now. He just needs to rest."

Even though Allen was kicked out of the group-therapy pro-gram, he did continue to meet with our family psychologist daily. Thom Rutledge talked to Allen and made sure he was working through his feelings before anything got out of control, and, of course, he made sure that Allen was regularly taking his meds. He was—I made sure of it. But that wasn't the problem. The prob-lem was that the medications made Allen feel terrible.

Every day, Allen suffered under the conflict of his depression medication. He was aware of how bad things had gotten, and he certainly didn't want to go back to that place, nor did he want to put a burden on us. But he didn't understand why something that was supposed to make him feel better also made him feel so bad.

Allen would take the drugs in the morning, and for a while, he'd be fully functional, engaging in conversation, maybe even telling a joke. Then, all of a sudden, he'd disappear to our room and throw himself across our bed or sit silently in a corner. He drew so far inward in those moments that it was hard for me to pull him back out. He knew that it was the drugs, that something wasn't right with his prescription, but whenever I asked him to tell me exactly how he was feeling, he struggled to find the words.

"I just don't feel . . . right," he would say. "Something about this isn't right."

When Allen finally went to meet with his new psychiatrist, a doctor recommended by Thom, I was thrilled that Allen would finally be able to get off the heavy-duty dosages he'd been pre-scribed in the hospital. I'd understood them as a necessary fix, but a temporary one. I also didn't need a single ounce of data to tell me that the medications Allen was on were not intended for long-term use. All I had to do was look at Allen. All I had to do was listen to his pain.

But the new psychiatrist didn't do that. He spent an hour with my husband and told him that everything was fine, that he should continue to take the same medication prescribed to him in the hospital and follow up in three more weeks.

When I heard the news from Allen, I flew into a rage. First, I called the psychiatrist and asked him to reconsider Allen's prescription. Then I called Thom and told him that Allen needed another referral, that he needed to see a doctor who would provide a more tailored approach to Allen's medical treatment.

"He keeps telling me that he's not feeling well," I told Thom. "I want to help him, but I'm not sure what I can do if we don't get him off of these drugs."

I was frantic, and Thom did his best to calm me down, reassuring me that this was a "process," that the psychiatrist Allen was seeing was one of the best in the city, that Allen would be fine.

So, I listened—not because I had full faith in Thom, but because I felt I had no choice. Ultimately, I think Allen felt the same way. He was sick of being sick, and as we approached Rosh Hashanah, the Jewish celebration of the new year, he wanted to believe that the coming year would be different, better. He *needed* to believe that. I know this because, months after he died, the boys found a copy of a speech that Allen had planned to deliver to our family on the first night of Rosh Hashanah.

> *Family—as you all know, the past few weeks have been particularly challenging for me. And consequently, for you guys too. I want to thank you for being here for me. I love you all.*
>
> *Rutledge tells me I'm on the mend, even though I am far from feeling 100 percent as I sit here with you right now.*

I'm choosing to trust him on that. I know that he has per-sonally battled with this depression monster too, and he tells me good things are to come. Fingers crossed.

I really need to address the fact that I feel so embarrassed by how out of control all of this has gotten. I don't even remember what happened in some cases. I do know that I landed in the hospital and that was no fun for me, and I know that that was difficult on you all too. I want to apolo-gize for all of that but Rutledge tells me I have nothing to apologize for.

What I am working on now, among many other things, is coming to terms with acceptance that I have this illness, this depression. Intellectually, I can get that this is an ill-ness like any other illness—diabetes, heart disease, what-ever—but in my gut it still feels like I am to blame, that I should be able to think my way out of this. I am working on believing that my having depression is not my fault and most importantly that it is an illness I have, not about per-sonal weakness.

So anyway, I am putting you guys on notice that this is hard work for me but I am going to be doing my best to hold my head up and not give into the temptation to stay in the shame. Be patient with me please, as you have been (Randi) and I promise that I am working on getting back to being the Allen you know—and if Rutledge really is telling me the truth, I'll hopefully even be a better version of me.

Thanks. I love you.

I can only assume that Allen didn't give his speech that night because Jonathan's girlfriend had come to dinner, and he wasn't ready to be vulnerable with anyone outside of our family. I understood and respected that, but when I read his speech, weeks after he intended to share it with me and the boys, giant tears began to fall from my eyes and onto the paper.

By then, I knew that things didn't actually get better, that he never had the chance to become that better version of himself he'd hoped to be. By then, Allen was long gone.

CHAPTER 20

I wish I could say that I felt good about leaving Allen behind when I went back to Atlanta the Monday after Rosh Hashanah began. I wish I could say that there wasn't a stabbing in my gut and a whisper in my . . . something—or somethings—telling me that maybe I shouldn't leave. I wish I could say that I thought he'd be perfectly fine without me because, if I'd thought that, I wouldn't have been filled with so much regret later.

———————

I'd stayed home for weeks with Allen, while he was in the hospital and after, canceling my trips to Atlanta and anything else that would take me away from him. When I was sick—whether I was having a piece of my pancreas removed or having a bag inserted into a hole in my colon, Allen was right there, never leaving my side. I'd always promised to return the favor, to love him in sickness and in health, but Allen was so strong, so resilient, that I'd never had the opportunity to repay the favor. Even when he was sick—on those days when getting out of bed must have felt tortuous, or the days when he struggled to find any reason to hope—he still put on a good face for me and the boys. But now he couldn't. Now the mask that he'd worn for decades had fallen free, the truth of his illness exposed.

At work, renovations on The Loft in Atlanta were finally complete, and we were entering our busiest season of fall weddings and holiday parties. I hadn't been working as much while caring for Allen, but I knew that the time was coming for me to step back in. Allen had always assumed full control of the business when I was incapacitated, ensuring that checks came in and bills got paid, that the company continued to thrive. Now it was my responsibility to do that for Allen while he recovered, but for that reason, I felt that I needed to remain by his side. At the very least, I felt that I needed to stay in the city instead of traveling to Atlanta for the first time in weeks.

My flight was scheduled to leave at noon, but early that Monday morning, I decided to call Thom. I was still on the fence, still happy to unpack my bag and cancel my trip at a moment's notice.

"Don't be ridiculous," he told me. "Allen will be fine, Randi. You need to get back to work; he needs to get back to work."

"Back to work? There's no way Allen should be working right now."

Thom sighed. "The best thing for Allen and you to do is to get back to normal as quickly as possible. You both need to have something else to focus on besides his sickness."

I wasn't convinced. I knew that Allen was still struggling with the meds he was on and was unable to focus on much of anything. There was no way he could go back to work. The question was: what would he do with all of his time if I went to Atlanta without him?

"I don't know," I told Thom. "I just don't feel really comfortable leaving him right now."

"What can I do to help you feel more at ease?" he said. "I'm happy to continue meeting with Allen every day while you're gone, and I will contact you immediately if I feel that something is amiss."

"Um . . . okay," I said finally. "I guess it'll be fine."

"It will be, Randi. Trust me."

The three days in Atlanta went by in a blur. I went back to The Loft and toured the space, making sure all of the final details remaining from the renovation were executed perfectly. I met with the sales team and discussed a plan to book events for the new year. I also spent a good amount of time with my team, getting updates on everything I'd missed from the previous weeks.

On Wednesday, I had lunch with my team before Cassidy and I were scheduled to fly back home. Most of the girls worked in the Atlanta office, but Cassidy had come down with me from Nashville, and her assistance had been invaluable. We talked over sandwiches and bowls of soup, but while I enjoyed spending time with them, I couldn't wait to get back home to Allen.

When we'd spoken the night before, Allen told me that he wasn't going to go to his therapy appointment, that he didn't think meeting with Thom was helping him. His words had crashed over me in a wave of anguish, and I begged him to reconsider. I told Allen that he had to go to therapy, that the boys and I needed him to. We went back and forth, but he ultimately agreed to go, even as his voice still dripped with uncertainty. We agreed that he would pick me up from the airport and that I would drop him off at therapy before popping into the office for a minute. Once his session was over, I'd pick him up and we'd go home together.

As the girls and I finished up lunch, I tried to push my concern for Allen from my mind. I wanted to believe that even though he didn't want to go to therapy, Thom was still right, that my leaving would actually be good for Allen, and I would return home to the man I'd married thirty years before.

Then, on my way to the airport, my phone rang, and my housekeeper's name flashed on the screen. I knew she was scheduled to come and clean the house that morning, but I didn't understand why she would be calling me. Maybe there was something going on in the house, I assumed, and Allen hadn't made it back home yet.

"I'm sorry, Mrs. Lesnick, but I can't clean your house today," she said once I'd answered.

"Why? Is the key not there? I left it where I always do."

"No, that's not it," she said. "There's just too many emergency vehicles on the street. I can't even drive up to your house."

It's ironic when I think about it now, how even after everything Allen had been through—from the breakdown to the hospitalization—I still didn't begin to consider that something else had happened to him. All I could think was that the house had burned down, or that maybe one of the dogs had bitten someone.

I hung up and immediately called Allen. Twice. I got no answer, so I called the boys next and told them to get to the house ASAP. Only then, as I was telling them that something may be wrong, that they needed to drop everything and get home, did I think about the last time I'd said that, on the night that changed everything.

My stomach was churning by then, my heart beating a quickened, nervous pace. My breathing was starting to get heavier, and I was starting to sense, deep inside, that something was very, very wrong.

I'd only been off of the phone for about a minute when it rang again. I felt it vibrate in my hand before I looked at the screen's caller ID, and in those moments before—those precious, hopeful, moments—I prayed that it would be Allen. It wasn't. It was my neighbor, Diane, a long-time friend who lived on the street.

As soon as I answered the phone, I could tell she'd been crying. Her voice was wild and distraught, and my worry only intensified.

"Randi!" she said between sobs, "they won't tell me anything! I've tried to talk to the police several times, but they won't tell me anything!"

The word "police" immediately tightened my stomach like a vise, but I took a deep breath and tried to maintain some semblance of composure. "Where are you now?" I asked.

"I'm standing across the street from your house," she said, with more sobs. "There are just so many people, Randi. They're every-where."

"Okay," I said. "Now, can you walk back over and tell one of the officers that I'd like to speak to them? Can you give him your phone so I can talk?"

She said yes, and while I waited, I sent up another prayer, asking for God to fix whatever could still be fixed, and to give me the strength to endure what couldn't.

Still, despite my prayer, I wasn't prepared for the message I received.

"Hello," the officer said when he came to the phone. "Is this Mrs. Lesnick?"

"Yes," I said, "this is Randi Lesnick. I live at the home you're at right now."

I held my breath as I waited for the officer to tell me what happened, and when he finally spoke again, my whole world collapsed.

"Your husband is dead," he said.

CHAPTER 21

What do you do when you hear that your husband is dead, and you are hundreds of miles away? Well, you panic and devolve into a hysterical rage, of course. You close your eyes while the earth spins quickly—too quickly—and you remind yourself to breathe. And, in my case at least, you thank God that someone is there to help you make it back home.

Cassidy immediately got on the phone with a few of my friends and tried to see if someone had a private plane that I could use to get back home faster. There were still hours left before my Southwest flight was scheduled to depart, and there was no way I could imagine sitting in one of those tiny, vinyl airport seats, staring at all the other passengers whose significant others were still alive, who were probably returning home after a vacation, or maybe visiting Nashville for a bachelorette party, maybe a tour of the Broadway Honky-Tonks.

We were fortunate enough to find someone who was willing to loan us their plane, but we quickly realized that the logistics just didn't make sense. They would have to file for a change in flight plan, reroute the plane from wherever it was to fly to Atlanta, and then refuel before it could take me to Nashville. This process would take hours, we discovered, and it would be no quicker than taking the commercial flight I was already booked on.

This is how Cassidy explained it to me, but, of course, I was not in the frame of mind to process anything. All I knew was that I wanted to be home right then. I wanted to wrap my arms around my sons; I needed to feel their warm, living bodies as a comfort, even as I knew they needed me to comfort them. I didn't want to give them the news over the phone. As I'd learned first-hand, tragedy isn't meant to be shared via cellular communication; it is, instead, the kind of thing that must be discussed in person, so you can look the other person in the eyes and try to cloak the harsh words with softness. I didn't realize that they already knew, that they were already at the house, standing in the wreckage of our past life without me.

The minutes and hours that unfolded next spread out like a heavy blanket, smothering me as the world went dark. In the months that have passed since then, I have searched my mind for remembrance, trying to understand how I made it through security and the airport concourse to make it onto the plane in Atlanta. How did I move through the airport surrounded by thousands of people who had no idea that I'd lost my husband and best friend? How did I manage to board the plane without collapsing into a heap of grief? How did I sit still during the duration of the flight without jumping from my feet and screaming and shouting and demanding that all that was wrong be made right? How did I make it through the hour-long flight when I knew there was nothing but pain waiting for me on the ground in Nashville? How did I deplane and walk through the BNA corridors—past the restaurants and shops and photos that all reminded me of home—when I knew that my husband wouldn't be there to greet me at baggage claim, that, in fact, I'd never see him alive again?

I still don't know how it all happened, only that Cassidy was there every step of the way, holding me up by my arm in case my legs failed under the weight of my shattered heart. She presented my boarding pass and ID and answered questions asked by well-meaning airline employees. On the plane, she sat next to me, whispering tender words of consolation, and assuring the worried flight attendants that I was okay, even though I clearly wasn't.

When we landed, Cassidy ushered me off the plane and out of the airport, where Natalie and Ashley, two of my employees, were waiting in a car to take me home. At the same time, two other girls from the Nashville office were waiting at baggage claim to pick up my luggage.

In the car, with agonizing silence filling the space around us, I held my breath as we rode to Franklin, to my dream home that was once so filled with life—and now the site of my husband's death.

I saw Jason first, his eyes red and wet, his shoulders slumped and shaking. I'd called him from Atlanta, before I even knew what had happened, and told him to rush home. When he arrived and saw all of the emergency vehicles, he immediately called Jon, who was busy setting up for an event with the Music City Tents and Events, the party rental company that had long been one of my favorite vendors. Joe Freidman, the owner of the company, was a good friend of our family, so when Jason told Jonathan he needed to drop everything and get home ASAP, Joe didn't hesitate to drive him.

That would have been bad enough—the boys arriving to an active crime scene with their mother still away in another state—but the negligence of the police officers on the scene only made things worse. After they located Allen's body, they found a suicide letter in his office. The letter was folded and stuffed into a white envelope; on the outside of it, my name was written in Allen's handwriting.

When Jason handed me the letter, I took note of the incoherency of Allen's words, how it seemed he'd typed it up in a flash of darkness, without thinking it through, without considering that maybe the moment would pass. It was so hard to make sense of it all, it was rambling and unorganized and when I tried to hear

Allen's voice in the sentences on the page, it was impossible. I couldn't find him there at all. But that wasn't what hurt me the most. Truly, the chaos of Allen's letter meant little compared to the fact that Jason and Jonathan had already read it, that the police officer had ignored my husband's instruction and given his last words to his vulnerable children first.

Jason and Jonathan have "grown up just like me," Allen wrote. *It is my fault they are disrespectful and have no manners. As the head of the family, I did them an injustice.*

My eyes met with Jason and Jonathan's when I read those lines, when I realized they'd read them too. There, in their eyes, was a mix of devastation and guilt, and there was nothing I could do to make it go away. It was bad enough that Allen had been too sick to see what an incredible father he was, that his last thoughts about his children were that he hadn't been good enough. What was worse was that Jason and Jonathan had been exposed to the lies that Allen was sick enough to believe.

By that point, our street was eerily quiet, the wailing sirens and flashing lights long gone. Even our house looked normal. There were no signs that my husband had taken his last breath just beyond our back door. His body had already been removed and carted off to the morgue, the place where they'd found him now perfectly ordinary to those who didn't know any better.

But Trixie and Duke, our dogs, knew. They were the only ones at home when Allen decided that he couldn't live another day in such pain. They must have seen him when he did it; now, they walked slow circles near the pool, whimpering and moaning where Allen's memory was still thick in the air.

My sister, Robin, and brother-in-law, Robert, were there too, along with Allen's cousin, Richard. I vaguely remembered calling my sister in the hysteria that transpired after I'd first gotten the news. Without a moment of hesitation, she'd headed to the airport immediately, hopping on the first flight from New York to Nashville and kickstarting a routine of selfless, unconditional support that continues to this day. I don't remember calling

Allen's cousin, but perhaps I did, and the veil of mourning I've been under has blocked this memory. Or perhaps Robin called, maybe the boys. I still am not sure, but I know that Robin, Robert, and Richard were on the same flight; together, they dropped what they were doing to come to Nashville and help us pick up the remnants of our lives.

But it would be a while before I was ready to do that.

———

I went to the funeral home the very next morning. We weren't able to bury Allen until October 7, four days after he killed himself, but in the meantime, I met with the director of the home.

When it was time to go in and see Allen—when I would finally have the chance to say goodbye to the man I'd loved for nearly three decades—I knew I couldn't do it alone. We walked in as a group, my sons and I, and I remember bracing myself for what I was sure would be a punch to my gut. I expected to see the Allen I'd left in Nashville when I traveled to Atlanta days before. I expected to see a man battered and broken, a man who'd finally given up. Instead, I saw a man who was relaxed, and at peace. I looked down at the smile on his face, and while it wasn't enough to push away the sorrow that was only beginning to cloud my vision, it was important. At the very least, I knew Allen's pain was gone.

There were so many people at my house when we got back—family, friends, and colleagues, so many people who knew Allen and wanted to be there for me and the boys as we grieved and tried to rebuild our lives without him. By that point, most everyone in the music industry knew that Allen had passed. News spreads like wildfire in a town as small as Nashville. Stories that ran in publications like MusicRow.com, *Billboard*, and the *Tennessean* only pushed things along, and the fact that I am so well-known and well-respected in the community helped too.

When the news made it to social media, hundreds of people left comments with their condolences, and many of them asked where they could send flowers or other gifts. We decided early that, in lieu of any memorial gifts, we wanted contributions to be made to the National Alliance of Mental Health. In the end, thousands of dollars were donated to the organization in Allen's name. I'd seen him struggle so much—from the time I met him, really, but especially in those final weeks, so if there was any way to use our loss as someone else's gain, to ensure that another person struggling with the depression got the help they really needed, that's what I wanted.

Ultimately, that didn't stop people from continuing to show up for me and our family. Paul Christensen, the CEO of Music and Sounds Records and a close friend and client, had enough food to feed twenty-five people catered every day for a week. Meanwhile, so many other people reached out personally just to offer their support. It was all so overwhelming, but in the most amazing, up-lifting way. Yes, I was the one who'd built the company, who was mostly responsible for rubbing elbows with music business big-wigs as I planned their number-one parties and holiday soirees. But even though it was my name on the sign outside of our office on Music Row, everyone still loved Allen.

People just gravitated to him. He was low-key but full of en-ergy, and in a world where people were known to say just what others wanted to hear, Allen was a welcome breath of honesty and transparency. There was no one who didn't enjoy sitting with Allen over coffee or a glass of wine and listening to him dispense much-needed advice, or just provide a listening ear. He'd done that for me since the beginning of our relationship, so it made me feel good to know that Allen had had as meaningful an impact on those around us.

Still, I hated that he wouldn't be around to talk to anymore. I hated that he wouldn't be around to talk me through business de-cisions or help me plan for the future. He wouldn't be around to meet our grandkids, and he wouldn't be there for me to retire and grow old with. These things were all I could think about as we prepared to say goodbye one final time.

CHAPTER 22

There was a porch on the back of our house in Franklin, a wide, comfortable space full of green plants that was known as my Zen room. In the days between Allen's death and the funeral, I spent most of my waking moments there, or in the family room, but instead of looking out into the backyard the way I used to with Allen, I kept the drapes drawn tight. I didn't want to see the pool or his man cave, the places that made me think of him. I certainly didn't want my mind to begin to form an image of my husband in his final, torturous moments.

For days and days, I just sat—not talking, and not really thinking about much, either, even as hundreds of people filed in and out of my house to pay their respects. They would pop their heads in and ask how I was doing, or if I needed help with anything. I just shook my head "no." The truth was, I didn't know how I was doing or what I needed. All I knew was that Allen was gone.

———

Allen's funeral was held at Congregation Micah, a synagogue in Brentwood with a beautiful, light-filled sanctuary. It was filled with people, so many people, but I couldn't see any of them. I could feel them and hear them; I knew they were there. But my only focus was on my dear Allen, his body laying at rest at the front of the room, and my two sons. They stood on either side of me—holding my hands, holding me up—as we made our way to the front row.

There were so many speakers, so many people with such wonderful things to say about Allen. They talked about his inquisitive nature, the way he wouldn't even buy a loaf of bread without doing hours of research beforehand. They talked about his resiliency, how he battled through depression for decades and never once let on that the fight was too much for him to handle. And they talked about his love for his family. One by one, Allen's friends and family looked down at Jason, Jonathan, and me and reminded us that Allen loved us more than anything else in the world, that he only left us when he did because he knew we'd be okay.

The tears were pouring down my face, my makeup streaked and eyeliner smudged, but their words comforted me. I knew they were right.

I will forever be in awe of Jason and Jonathan for the courage they showed in standing up to speak. They were the epitome of grace and strength as they stood to comfort others even as they were struggling to fight through their own despair. I'd been asked to speak as well, but there was no way that I could. How could I form even one coherent sentence when nothing but sobs came out each time I opened my mouth?

I couldn't, and I knew that. But I also knew that I had plenty to say about my husband. As each day passed, I was missing him more, but it was the little things that I clung to most. Reading the newspaper together doesn't seem like such a big deal until you can't anymore. Ordering in Chinese food isn't such a momentous occasion until you realize it won't happen ever again. Suddenly, my mind shifted from thoughts about his illness and his last days and what drove him to leave us too soon. Now, all I could think about were all the moments in between—the times where we were just Allen and Randi: parents, friends, lovers, and business partners.

This is the Allen that I wanted everyone, including myself, to remember. So, I wrote up a short speech and gave it to my sister to read for me during the funeral.

My Dearest Allen,

You were my best friend, my sounding board, my partner in business, and my life partner. You will always be the love of my life.

I can remember traveling around the country watching Jon play hockey and you banging on the glass every time a shot was missed. I couldn't sit with you then because you were impossible to enjoy a game with. I only wish I had one more game with you.

I remember our favorite trips to Knoxville to watch Jason march before a UT game. I only wish I had one more weekend with you in Knoxville.

You were my partner in our company and we fought over our differences of opinion of how things should be run. I only wish I had one more argument with you.

We know you were in pain and you were not in a logical frame of mind, or you would have never left us. We are angry that you have left us alone but know you are now out of pain and at peace. It may be too late for you to realize how much you were loved but if you are looking down and can see the love and pain in this room, you will realize all the lives you have touched. I love you and your children love you and we wish we had one more time with you.

Allen's funeral was on October 7, and we continued to sit shiva until the tenth. Jason, Jonathan, and I wore black ribbons that were pinned on our clothes by the rabbi and ripped to represent the giant tears in our heart. The tradition is to do nothing but mourn—no cooking, no cleaning, no reading or watching TV.

This was easy for me, of course, and after the funeral, I decided to move from my position on the back porch to my bedroom. Most of the time, I just lay in bed, careful not to disturb the pillows or the blanket on Allen's side. To this day, I sleep only on my half of the bed, leaving his side untouched.

To be clear, I've never been so disillusioned to think Allen was coming back—I knew he was gone just as sure as I knew that I might never get over his passing—but I wanted to preserve as much as I could. I wanted him to know that even if he had to leave us, I would still honor and respect the place he'd held in our lives and our home.

The night of the funeral, my sister poked her head into the room and told me that the rabbi had come, that I needed to get dressed and come to meet her. She wanted to help us find closure by having friends and family who were there say some nice things about Allen. I sat on a chair and I looked around at everyone, their eyes watery and downcast, escaping contact with mine.

It was a surreal moment, similar to what happened at the gravesite in the moments after Allen's body was lowered into the dirt. There were so many people there, lines and lines of them making their way to shovel dirt onto Allen's grave, their tears making tracks down their own faces, their hands clenched tight into balls of frustration and sadness. I remember watching them and feeling my heart rate quicken, like the blue sky above was starting to collapse around me. I couldn't breathe, and I told Jason to take me away.

In my living room, I felt like that all over again. I didn't want "closure." It was too early for "closure." Allen's shoes and socks were still strewn across the bedroom floor; his towel was still hanging in the bathroom. I still felt him all around me, and I didn't want to get out of bed because I knew that that wouldn't help me see him, touch him, talk to him ever again. And there was nothing that anyone in that room could say to change that.

I needed time. I needed time to be mad and sad and hurt and confused. I needed to mourn my husband in the only way I knew how, so I got up from chair, ran into my bedroom, and slammed the door shut behind me.

CHAPTER 23

As shiva wore on, with all our family and friends still in town for the funeral, I began longing to be alone. By the Friday after the funeral, the noise was too much, the constant fussing over the boys and me—assuring us that everything would be fine and shoving a Xanax in my mouth at the first sight of a breakdown—was smothering. I wasn't completely sure that I was ready to try to figure out life on my own, but at the very least, I wanted to be able to cry in peace or skip lunch and not have people thinking that I was trying to starve myself.

Conversely, I was also afraid of being alone. Once the remaining food had been wrapped up and stored in the freezer and the house had grown eerily silent, I would be forced to navigate the seven thousand square feet of my home without the person who was supposed to live there with me forever.

The boys would still be there—Jason living in the basement and Jonathan open and willing to visit whenever I needed him—but their presence wouldn't repair the massive rips in my heart. If anything, seeing them would remind me of how much Allen loved them and had dedicated his life to being the type of father he wished he'd had. I worried that seeing our sons would always make me miss Allen even more.

Ever since Allen died, I'd felt like I was suspended on this emotional roller coaster, wishing I had even five more minutes with him but also wondering how long I would be paralyzed by memories of him, memories that made it difficult to put one foot in front of the other, or breathe in and out.

Allen was gone, yes, but he was also all around me. I had my morning coffee without him, but I drank the brand and flavor he'd bought; every time I opened my cabinet I reached past his favorite mug. The constant reminders were all too much, and all at once, I couldn't take it anymore.

On the last night of shiva, Debbie, a friend of my sister, Robin, clasped a hand around mine and looked deep into my eyes that were still—as always—wet with tears. I was tired of being coddled, of people feeling sorry for me, but I felt my body relax next to hers. She asked me how I was doing, and I told her the truth. I told her that I was beginning to feel as though the end of Allen's life had signaled the end of mine. I didn't want it to be like that. I felt, in my heart, that Allen wanted me to be happy, that he probably thought that leaving this earth would ease some sort of burden on me and make things easier for me. He was wrong.

Being happy again was such an impossibility that I didn't expect or consider it. I just wanted to not feel so sad, to not wake up already counting the minutes until I could crawl back in bed again at the end of the night. But that felt impossible too.

"You need to get away," Debbie said to me. "You're living in the house where you lived with Allen . . . and where Allen died. Of course you're having a hard time."

I nodded silently and pushed back a fresh wave of tears.

"I have a house in Naples," Debbie continued. "Maybe you and the boys should go down for a while. Stay for a long weekend; get some fresh air and get away from all of the reminders."

I nodded again and wiped the tears that were now streaming down my cheeks. It was the last night of shiva, and Jason, Jonathan, and I decided that we would leave first thing the next morning.

———

The house was beautiful and spacious with an open floor plan and windows that looked out onto a screened-in pool. Under normal circumstances, we would have spent as much time as possible at the beach, soaking in the sun as we played cards and talked about work and life. But these circumstances were far from normal. We went to dinner a couple of nights, and while the boys spent hours in the pool, I sat beside it, unwilling to fully immerse myself in the water. For the most part, though, we were merely going through the motions, each of us unable to find the words to communicate what we still didn't understand.

There were enough rooms for each of us to have our own, but Jason and Jonathan were together most nights, seeking comfort in one another in a way I hadn't seen since they were kids. As for me, I spent the nights staring at the ceiling above my bed until my eyelids were too heavy to stay open on their own. I worked overtime to keep my mind completely clear, lest my thoughts drift back to Allen and the wretched reality I'd suddenly found myself in.

I wasn't thinking about what awaited me back in Nashville, how I'd be able to wake up day after day in the house we'd built together. I wasn't even thinking about the business. We were heading into our busiest time of year, with the Country Music Awards and the holidays just weeks away, but I couldn't imagine putting my mind on table designs or floral arrangements. All I could think about was surviving from one moment to the next. One step at a time was all I could manage.

———————

By early November, Jason, Jonathan, and I were each heading back to work, all of our energy channeled toward creating our new normal.

My first big event was a CMA party for Music and Sounds. Paul and I were great friends and had worked together for so long that my team could handle this event with our eyes closed and both hands tied behind our backs. We knew their style and aesthetic; we knew every detail that needed to be executed and how to do it well. The problem was that Chloe, a former employee, had left my company seven months before to go and work for Paul as his assistant.

To be clear, I wasn't upset that Chloe had left—I was happy that she'd found a position that she felt would better position her to achieve her long-term goals—but I quickly noticed that she had a problem separating her previous job from her current one. She worked for me long enough to understand the Music and Sounds account as well as any of us, and even though she was now working directly for Music and Sounds, she couldn't resist the urge to act as if she was still sitting on the other side of the table. She kept trying to take over the planning, stepping on our toes and frustrating my employees in the process.

The event was to be held at the Bell Tower, and after receiving an email from the venue that expressed their concern about receiving direction from both us and Chloe, I sat down at my desk and decided to reach out to Paul so that we could get the issue settled once and for all. It was my first day back in the office, and I wanted—I *needed*—as little drama as possible. In an email, I forwarded the message I'd received from Bell Tower and, above it, wrote one sentence: "What am I supposed to do with this?"

Moments later, Chloe was calling me, pleading her case. "I'm not doing anything wrong," she said. "I'm just trying to make sure everything is perfect, and I don't understand why you're treating me like this!"

"Excuse me, but I sent a personal email directly to Paul," I said, ignoring her accusations. "Why are you responding to it?"

For the next five minutes, she whined and complained and asked me why I was "being so mean to her." I took deep breaths and tried to calmly explain that my company was hired to do a job—a job that my company had been doing since she was in elementary school—and that she needed to take a step back and focus on being Paul's assistant instead of micromanaging my staff. It didn't work.

"Look, Chloe," I said finally. "I'm going through a lot right now, and I really need to take a break here. We'll just have to talk about this later."

I didn't wait for her to respond before pressing the "end" button. I was only weeks removed from losing my husband, from losing my best friend in the whole world, and I didn't want to argue with anyone, and certainly not about an awards show party.

I sat my phone on my desk and tried to think happy thoughts. The girls in the office obviously knew about Allen, but they didn't know that every day was just as difficult as the day before, that I was still so far from being able to "move on." I didn't want them to know because, if they did, they would send me right back home and tell me that I shouldn't be working, that they had everything handled. They were right about having everything handled. They didn't need me, even though I desperately needed them, needed work, needed the routine of a day in the office to keep my mind off of everything else.

I took one more deep breath and was about to ask the girls about going out for lunch when my phone rang again. I thought it was Chloe and was prepared to press the button that would send her directly to voicemail, but when I picked it up, I saw Paul's name flash across the screen.

"Chloe's upset," he said when I answered.

"I know, but I just really can't deal with that right now," I said. "It's my first day back, and I have a lot going on."

"Well, I have a lot going on too, and now Chloe's crying." He paused, sighed. Then he added, "And since she's crying, you're fired."

If not for the fact that my life had already been completely up-ended over the prior month, I wouldn't have even believed the words that came out of Paul's mouth. We'd known each other for decades, and never once had he ever fired me from a job. We'd even gone into business together and never had a problem.

But if nothing else, Allen's death had taught me that nothing was certain, that anything and everything could change in the blink of an eye.

"Whatever, Paul," I said into the phone. Then I tossed it into my purse, walked out of the office, got into my car, and drove home.

I'd wanted so badly to get on with my life, to show everyone, including myself, that I could make it on my own. But now I was less sure than ever that I actually could. Had Paul fired me just two months before, Allen would have talked me through it and calmed me down with ease. He would have told me that Chloe was just overly emotional because she was trying to prove herself at her new job. He would have reminded me about the depths of my relationship with Paul, about the seeds we'd planted that had grown roots too deep to be pulled after one miscommunication. Allen would have told me that I had other things to worry about anyway, that everything would work itself out just like it always did, and even though I would have still been upset, I would have nodded and told him that he was right. Then we would have ordered Chinese food for good measure.

But now Allen was gone, and now there was no one to tell me all the things he would have said. Now, I could only race down I-40 toward Franklin, past the retail stores and overly anxious homeowners who were beginning to welcome the approaching holiday season far sooner than I would have liked.

The weather in Nashville had taken its final turn toward autumn. No longer threatened by temps that hovered in the sixties, the days were perpetually cool, the nights alone in my bed now downright cold. Christmas was still a month-and-a-half away, but we were only weeks out from Thanksgiving, and the very thought of it brought physical pain. I hadn't considered the holidays without Allen, and as I pulled into our driveway and my eyes took in the empty porch swing where Allen and I had sat on so many fall afternoons, all I could do was sob. I knew then that I had absolutely nothing to be thankful for.

CHAPTER 24

I f losing Allen wasn't already hard enough—and it was, it was the most difficult thing I've ever experienced in my life—losing him just before the holidays was a special kind of torture that I wouldn't wish on my worst enemy. I've always loved Thanksgiving, Christmas, and the month between them, the red-and-green explosion of secret Santas, carols, and Hallmark movies.

Allen and I would shop for the boys and each other, pretending to not know what we were getting even though we'd both divulged our wish list weeks before. And then there was the food, so much glorious food. Every Thanksgiving, I made turkey and all the fixings: the stuffing, candied yams, and green bean casserole. Christmas typically involved some kind of roast, maybe a casserole, and throughout the month of December there was an endless supply of desserts. Cakes and cookies and pies, some store-bought, others homemade, Allen's favorite and mine too.

For many people, the holidays are a time for relaxing, for long, leisurely days viewing the Christmas displays at Cheekwood Botanical Garden while sipping on a hot peppermint mocha. With a schedule that was always jam-packed during the last two months of the year, I never really had time to rest, but the holidays were rejuvenating, nonetheless. Everywhere you looked there was happiness and cheer, so many sweet reminders of the joy of family.

But there would be no joy for our family at the end of 2019. As the dust began to settle after shiva, the trip to Florida, and the spat with Paul, I couldn't imagine going through the motions of the holiday season. Not without Allen. I couldn't pretend that there was so much to be thankful for when, at the time, all I could see was loss and pain. I was hurting and the boys were hurting, and the gaping hole in our lives that Allen left behind was proof that he had been hurting too. He'd sat with his struggles for decades, waiting them out and praying that he wouldn't be overtaken, that maybe some new therapist or prescription could make him feel closer to whole. Yet nothing ever worked.

So, we let the holidays come and go, and refused to acknowledge them. First came Jason's birthday on November 14, and while we would normally go out for dinner and have a few friends over for drinks and cake, we stayed in by ourselves. As a mother, I didn't want my son to think that he no longer mattered just because his father was gone, but I couldn't bring myself to celebrate. Ultimately, Jason didn't want to celebrate either, perhaps because he knew that his brother's most recent birthday hadn't been the same either. Allen was in the hospital when Jonathan turned twenty-five; in our hopefulness for the future, we'd visited bringing birthday cake and bright smiles, by November the hope and smiles were long gone.

We couldn't control the calendar or the hands of time that kept pushing forward, but we could certainly dictate what we did on those days. We could refuse to treat each day as normal, as if nothing had changed when, in fact, everything had.

Thanksgiving came and went next, then Christmas and New Year's. And while other families were gathering around their fireplaces with mugs of cider and perfectly wrapped presents, the boys and I were trying to gather the pieces of ourselves that remained and figure out how to put them back together again.

We canceled our New Year's Eve party, our annual feast of stone crab flown in from Florida, steaks, potatoes, and stuffed tomatoes that we loved to share with friends. At the end of 2018, our good friends Kevin and Dayla had come to celebrate with

Allen and me, along with Jason and his girlfriend. In December 2019, after Allen was gone, Kevin and Dayla reached out, offering to fly into town and continue the tradition in Allen's stead. They said it would help me find some sense of normalcy, but I couldn't imagine continuing a tradition without Allen that he and I had started together.

Perhaps it was the resiliency of youth, but Jason and Jonathan were the ones who took the first tangible steps on our new path without Allen. I'd still been living in the bedroom that carried so much of Allen and his memory. I was still careful to maintain my space on my side of the bed without disrupting his. His shaving cream and toothbrush were still on the bathroom counter, his favorite shampoo still sitting in the corner of the shower. And his clothes were still everywhere, hanging in his closet, folded neatly in his drawers. These constant reminders of Allen were difficult to see, but they were also difficult to remove. Despite the pain of their continued existence, I was somehow sure that the pain of removing them would be even greater.

Jason and Jonathan didn't tell me that they were planning to clear out all of Allen's old things. They must have known that I would have stopped them, that I would have laid myself across the floor of our closet like a thirtysomething woman objecting to the demolition of her childhood home. So, they waited until I left for work and then began meticulously packing away their father's belongings. They weren't planning to permanently get rid of anything, at least not yet, but the boys knew that Allen's things needed to be out of my line of sight, that Allen would have wanted me to be strong without him and being surrounded by all his stuff was making that increasingly difficult.

As Jason and Jonathan gathered shoes and socks, cuff links and handkerchiefs, and placed them in boxes and totes, they also came across other items—receipts and invoices and scraps of paper with Allen's handwriting scrawled across them. When I got home from work the day they'd begun clearing out our room, Jason was holding a piece of paper in his hand, his face drained of color and emotion.

It was obvious that he'd already read it several times over, but he didn't tell me what it said, where he'd found it, or how the words on the page would rock me to my core. Instead, he handed it to me and said, "This was Dad, not the letter he wrote the day he died. This is how I'm going to remember him."

I'd missed it on my first read-through, but when I saw it—and understood it—tears began pouring from my eyes. Allen had intended to give his speech on the first night of Rosh Hashanah, just one day before I left for Atlanta the last time . . . just hours before I would see Allen for the last time.

My mind went back to the conversations I'd had with Rutledge before I left, to his assurances that Allen would be okay, that me going back to work would actually be helpful. I'd questioned him then, and even after Allen's death. But reading about the pain that my husband was obviously still in shed an especially bright light on what was beginning to feel like negligence on Rutledge's part. I'd trusted him, both to take care of my husband and to keep me abreast of his progress—or lack thereof. But I couldn't help but think that he'd done neither.

It was not Allen's admission of embarrassment about his breakdown or the fact that he was far from feeling 100 percent healthy that twisted my stomach into knots. It was his stated trust of Rutledge, a trust that I also shared, a trust that was ultimately breached.

While still holding Allen's speech in my hands, I let my brain swirl with questions. What if I had overlooked some sign from Allen that Rutledge wasn't the best therapist for him? What if the years Allen had spent working with Rutledge had come at the expense of Allen actually getting better? And, finally, what if I had trusted my gut and not left Allen at home while I went back to Atlanta?

I had no answers to any of these questions, of course. All I had was more pain and more guilt, yet another reason to feel that there was very little light at the end of the long, dark tunnel stretching out before me.

As 2019 bled into 2020, I had no clue about the impending pandemic, how the whole world would shut down around us and add an unyielding sense of isolation and loneliness on top of my still raw grief. All I knew was that I was ready, finally, for something different. I needed change—big change—if I was ever going to be able to live without Allen. I was unsure about the months that lay ahead and the sheer amount of change that I would have to undertake, but I knew where to start.

It was time to move out of my dream home, to say goodbye to the home that Allen and I had built together.

CHAPTER 25

I closed on my new condo in downtown Nashville on December 28, 2019. It had all happened so fast. One day I was riding around town with my sister, trying to find a place that felt like me—the newly widowed me—and the next day I had a shiny, new three-bedroom condo that was about a third the size of my Franklin home.

In retrospect, I think it was the differences that attracted me. The Franklin house was seven thousand square feet with plenty of outdoor space and a pool, while the condo was about sixteen hundred square feet with a patio that was little more than twice the length of Duke and Trixie's bodies. This arrangement would never work, I soon realized, but on the day I visited, I just remember thinking about how it was nothing like the home I already had—nothing like the home Allen and I had built together. And for that reason alone, I was all-in.

I had already let Jason know that I was thinking about getting rid of the house, that he'd have until February or so to find somewhere else to live. The deadline was relatively arbitrary, but it was far enough away that I would have time to pull the pieces of myself together and mentally prepare to leave the home I thought I'd spend the rest of my life in. At the same time, it wasn't so quick that I would have to rush through the process. As it was, the boys didn't want me to sell it. They missed their father, and for them, staying close to Allen meant staying in the space he'd left behind, walking in his footsteps and following the road he'd paved.

But that just wasn't an option for me. If there was any hope for me to make something of my remaining years, to not be swallowed by the grief of losing my husband as well as the future I thought we'd share, I needed to start fresh. I needed to be in a place that didn't smell like Allen, that didn't have his spirit seeping from the baseboards. I felt guilty about this, of course. I didn't want to upset my sons, nor did I want them to think that I was trying to run away from the memory of my husband—even though, on many days, it felt like I was. If I didn't run away, if I didn't leave behind the life I'd had with Allen, I didn't know how I'd ever be able to find a new one on my own. Meanwhile, I was still left floundering in limbo. I knew that I needed to leave but I couldn't, not yet anyway, so stretching the timeline into the new year seemed like a reasonable compromise.

Meanwhile, as soon as I got the keys to the condo, I started ordering furniture and having it delivered to the new place. I bought new sofas and chairs and a dining room table with more than enough chairs for my family that was now just three. I ordered a new bed and a desk for my office, plus drapes, towels, and brand-new kitchenware. The only things that I wanted to bring from the old house were my clothes, a few pieces of art that Allen and I had collected together, and pictures of the boys from when they were growing up. Everything else would stay.

I didn't even want to be responsible for clearing the old house of the old things from my old life, so I hired a company to do it for me. They were instructed to sell everything in the house and to give the leftover to Goodwill. For the first time in my life, I didn't even think about getting the best deal—I didn't discuss sale prices for the TVs or the crystal or the unopened bottles of vintage wine. I just wanted it gone and planned to treat the net proceeds like a life-support payment: a financial gain made possible by tremendous loss.

This was the plan that gave me the slightest sense of relief, for with it, I began to feel that I was taking control again. Losing my husband may have been out of my hands, but at least I could decide how I would let it affect me going forward.

Then, as January gave way to February and move-out day drew nearer, I felt my heart began to seize with anxiety. By that point, I was mentally prepared to leave the house behind, and I was mentally prepared to part with all of the things gathered over decades of life and marriage. But I suddenly realized that I didn't want to be there to witness it when it all happened—when some young couple offered to purchase the four-poster bed that Allen and I had spent so many nights in, or when the first offer was made on my dream house, the house I thought I'd spend forever in.

It was days before Valentine's Day, and if the estate sale wasn't enough to drive me out of town, the impending celebration of love was the final push I needed. Valentine's Day always, always meant time alone with Allen. He did the traditional gifts and chocolates, but it was the words we shared on that day that always meant the most to me. Each year we talked about our love for each other—our marriage and our family—and where we wanted to see ourselves in the years to come. For the first time in nearly thirty years, I wouldn't be spending my Valentine's Day with Allen, and the thought frightened me to my core. There was no way I could be alone.

I booked a flight to New York and decided to spend the holiday with my sister and her family. When I arrived, Robin and I went to dinner and watched movies and tried to pretend that everything was okay—normal even—but mostly I stared out the window of her guest bedroom and replayed the last conversation I'd had with Allen on a loop. Had I been nice enough? Sympathetic enough? When he thought about his last interaction with me, was he happy? Had I been the wife he needed me to be?

Hour after hour I tortured myself like this, and as I ate steak and sipped red wine on February 14, I told myself to get used to that feeling. God had already given me my greatest love. Now that Allen was gone, I could feel deep within that I would never love again.

Three days later, my plane touched down back in Nashville and, after having already received word that everything in the Franklin house had been sold and there was already an offer to purchase the property, I beelined straight to the condo, vowing to never visit the house again. For months, I had been trying to envision my new normal, and now was the time to live it. No more excuses; no more stalling. I had to get comfortable in my new life in my new home, in a new world without Allen.

Little did I know that just two weeks after traveling to New York, that new world would shut down completely.

———————

There is never a "right" or "better" time to lose your husband, but I can guarantee it's not just before a global pandemic, when all of the world suddenly finds itself isolated and alone.

As the coronavirus settled over our city, I was emotionally wrecked. All the events we had on the books were pushed to 2021 or cancelled outright. In seeing that we were probably in for a long ride, many of my employees quit and decided to move back home with their parents in other cities. For those who remained, I bought them laptops and sent them home to work remotely. Initially, I retained enough staff to maintain the business; the problem was that there was no business to maintain. A PPP loan kept our heads above water for a short while, but it wasn't long before I had to find a way to stop bleeding cash.

Selling my Music Row office was an easy way to lower monthly expenses while also providing a temporary financial cushion as we continued to move forward into the coronavirus unknown. Still, the decision was a heartbreaking one to make. Purchasing that building meant, for me, that I had arrived, that I'd claimed my rightful place in Nashville's music industry. Selling it felt like I'd lost that place, just like I'd lost so much else.

Meanwhile, Jason and Jonathan were dealing with their loss in the best ways they knew how, which is to say that, initially at least, they weren't dealing with it at all. I started therapy soon after I returned from New York, and it was as much about having someone to talk to as it was about working through my grief. My therapist and I connected weekly over Zoom, a testament to the disconnected world we were now living in. The screens were awkward at first, but eventually I looked forward to logging in, to having at least an hour to speak freely about the fog I was still under.

Initially, neither of the boys were interested in therapy, despite my encouragement. After their father's suicide, they justifiably questioned its value and preferred to embark on their healing journey alone. It wasn't until I sent Jason to pick up mail from the Franklin house that he changed his mind. I knew my own emotional frailty and thus refused to go, but Jason said he could handle it, that he would grab the envelopes and packages and come right back, no problem. And it wouldn't have been a problem if he hadn't looked toward the patch of land where our family swing once sat, the bench with two seats that rocked back and forth from its free-standing frame. It had been sold along with everything else, and the emptiness of the space triggered the longing in Jason that he'd been attempting to sweep past for months.

After emptying the mailbox and racing back to my condo, he threw the mail on the kitchen bar and, with tears pouring from his eyes, said, "Please don't ever make me go back there again!"

I nodded and wrapped my arms around him, and when his sobs began to quiet, he whispered that he was finally ready to talk to someone. As for Jonathan, all I could do was trust that he would come to me when he was ready, that, in the meantime, the pain from losing his father wouldn't eat him alive.

———

By June, I'd come to realize that my downtown condo, while beautiful, could not be my forever home. Duke and Trixie were spending all their time indoors and suffering as a result, and I felt the same. The walls grew closer and closer each day; at the same time, any hope of forging new relationships with my neighbors was dashed by their frustration about my restless dogs. At least once a week, someone was knocking on the door and asking if I could quiet them down. My heart broke for them and for me, and I set out, once again, to find the place where we could begin again.

When my sister had driven me around Nashville to find a new place in the weeks after Allen's death, I had little concern for details or amenities. I just knew that I needed something different, something far from Franklin. But now, in the spring of 2020, I was beginning to settle into my new life as a single, widowed woman, and that absolutely impacted the way I viewed potential homes. I wanted more square footage and more outdoor space, sure, but I also wanted a community. Without Allen, I actually *needed* a community. Allen had always been my rock and my protector; the one person I knew I could count on no matter what I was going through. Now that he was gone, I worried about what would happen if I ever got sick and didn't have him to care for me.

In the fall of 2020, I was thrilled—and somewhat surprised—to learn that I could, in fact, make it without Allen. Despite constant handwashing, mask-wearing, and every other recommended behavior meant to prevent a COVID-19 infection, I was diagnosed with the illness on December 8.

My mind had been racing with worst-case scenarios and the stories of all the people who'd contracted COVID since March but weren't successful in overcoming it, but it was the physical toll of the illness that weighed the heaviest. I will never forget stepping out of my bathroom and having my muscles grow so suddenly weak that I was sent crashing to the floor. I couldn't stand or pull myself up, and my recent diagnosis ensured that I was all alone.

It took hours, but I was finally able to drag myself over to the bed where my phone was sitting. I picked it up and called my neighbor Leanne, a friendly woman whom I'd known for about five months but who was kind as any lifelong friend. I told her what happened and with desperation dripping on every word, asked her to put on gloves and three masks—to drape herself in a garbage bag if she had to—because I had fallen and needed help getting onto my bed. She arrived to help me minutes later, and throughout the rest of my quarantine, she and my other neighbors dropped off casseroles, quarts of soup, and everything else I needed.

Even now, I am overwhelmed with gratitude for the kindness of the strangers who welcomed me into their community and embraced me as one of their own. Likewise, I am grateful to God for the nudge to purchase this house, in this community, on this street. I can't imagine what would have happened to me if I had collapsed in the condo or had moved somewhere else where the people were far less willing to care for a highly contagious widow.

Still, each day feels a bit better than the last, and I am not as afraid of the future as I was back in October of 2019. I suppose that's enough, at least for now. In the early months after Allen's death, I wasn't sure I'd ever get to the point where I could see a future without him, where I wouldn't wake up each day and want to immediately close my eyes again and keep them shut.

Now, my eyes are wide open, and I am starting to see again. I am starting to see that I can cook dinner for one, put up a Christmas tree on my own, and even sleep alone in a bed meant for two. Most importantly, I am starting to see that even though I don't want to live without Allen, I can.

I can. I must. And I *will*.

ACKNOWLEDGMENTS

Cassidy, for getting me home from Atlanta after I heard the news.

Dayla and Kevin, for being my and Allen's closest friends and for continuing to be there for me and the boys.

Diane and Steve, for being such wonderful friends to Allen and me throughout the years.

John and Megan, for your ongoing support.

Liz and Jim, for checking on me every day since Allen passed away, since they knew I was afraid to be alone.

And most of all to my friends in the Del Webb on Lake Providence, for welcoming me into their community and opening my eyes so I can see again.

ABOUT THE AUTHOR

Randi Lesnick went to college for one semester before going to work at her mother's agency. She embarked on an adventure in the hotel business, which took her to Las Vegas, Miami, Anchorage, Dallas, and eventually home to New York where she met the love of her life, Allen.

The two made Tennessee their home, and Randi has been an event planner for twenty-five years and has met some of the most famous people in the world. Throughout her success, Allen remained at her side. He was her friend, he was her lover, he was her partner. Randi loves where she lives now and she loves the friends she has but she will always miss her husband. One foot in front of the other and one step at a time!

This is Randi's first book.